The Ultimate
Irish Cookbook

111 Dishes From Ireland To Cook Right Now

Slavka Bodic

Please sign up for free Balkan and Mediterranean recipes:
www.balkanfood.org

Introduction

Do you want to celebrate the authentic Irish flavors by cooking some delicious and savory meals at home? Then you have found a right fit for you! This cookbook will introduce you to some of the most popular Irish recipes and meals that you'll definitely love, especially if you're a foodie. Whether you've been to Ireland or not, you can recreate its traditional cuisine at home with the help of this comprehensive cookbook. Ireland is popular for its unique culture, languages, and food; thus, this book is one good way to come close to the flavorsome cuisine of this European region.

The Ultimate Irish Cookbook will introduce Irish cuisine and its culinary culture in a way that you may have never tried before. It brings you a variety of Irish recipes in one place. The cookbook is great for all those who always wanted to cook Irish food on their own, without the help of a native Irish. As a result of this Irish cuisine cookbook, you can create a complete Irish menu of your own, or you can try all the special Irish recipes on different occasions as well. In this cookbook, you'll find popular Irish meals and ones that you might not have heard of formerly.

In these recipes, you'll also find some of the most commonly used Irish ingredients like Guinness beer and lots of veggies and meat. Not only that, but you'll also learn how to make such ingredients and use them in different meals. The Irish cuisine has been comprised of various dishes of the Irish people and has been widely spread across the globe. There's a clear difference between taste and flavor in the food of various regions of Ireland due to the differences in culture and diverse geological locations. And in this cookbook, you'll discover all the recipes from different parts of Ireland.

What you can find in this cookbook:
- Insights about Ireland and Irish Cuisine
- Irish Breakfast recipes
- Snacks and Appetizers
- Salads and Soups
- Main Dishes
- Irish Desserts and drinks

Let's try all these Irish recipes and recreate a complete menu to celebrate the amazing Irish flavors and lovely aromas.

Table of Contents

Why Irish Cuisine?

What does Irish cuisine remind you of? Does it trigger delicious, boxty pancakes made from potatoes, and, or does it conjure the Irish coffee? Well, the cuisine has tons of other exciting and delicious meals to offer you. It has a mix of regional and cultural influence, which makes Irish food not only special but also quite unique. Irish food attracts many fans because of the amazing combination of vegetables, meats, and fruits it offers.

When it comes to Irish meals, they're made using basic spices, more fermented food and a lot of fruits and vegetables. Most meals are loaded with a number of ingredients. The cuisine focuses on the use of all type of meat, poultry, seafood, vegetables, and other agricultural produce. Some fruits and veggies are widely grown in Ireland, like potatoes, and that's the reason that potatoes are most commonly used in most Irish meals. Similarly, cabbage, sauerkraut, berries, and apples are some popular ingredients in this region. Other commonly used ingredients of Irish cuisine are:

- Potatoes
- Beef
- Pork
- Peppers
- Beets
- Cabbage
- Sauerkraut
- Corned beef

- Carrots
- Celery
- Butter
- Mushrooms

Irish dishes are known for their unique tastes and aromas. There are several dishes that are worth trying on this cuisine, like:

- Beef Stew with Cheddar Dumplings
- Irish Cabbage and Bacon
- Irish Cheddar Macaroni Cheese
- Dublin Coddle
- Maple Mustard Corned Beef
- Bacon Corned Beef Burgers

For desserts and beverages, there are several good options to choose from, like the Orange Whiskey Soufflé Pie, Plum Pudding Cake, Sticky Toffee Pudding, Shamrock Cookies, Irish Oat Flapjacks, etc.

Ireland

Ireland has always been an important attraction in Europe. In retrospect, it remained away from the center of Europe; thus, most of its beauty is completely untapped. The whole island is divided into two parts, Northern Ireland, which is the part of the United Kingdom, and the independent state known as the Republic of Ireland. What most of us aren't familiar with is the diversity of its cuisine, culture and amazing people. The region is packed with amazing landscapes and beautiful heritage sites. Irish universities and education institutes attract millions of students from around the world.

The country covers an area of 32,595 square miles (84,421 square kilometers) with a population of more than 4.8 million people in the Republic of Ireland, while around 1.8 million people living in Northern Island (UK). Irish culture has left an important influence on other European cultures in the field of literature. Mainstream Western Irish culture, a strong indigenous culture, t is expressed through Gaelic games, Irish language and Irish music. Ireland's culture shares many characteristics with Great Britain, including the English language and sports like rugby, horse racing, football, and golf.

People who have never been to Ireland and never explored many of its places and cities cannot fathom the beauty of its breathtaking landscapes. Most people get the idea of this land from the movies they watch, but Ireland is much more than what you see in pictures and videos. It has some gorgeous cities and diversely populated urban centers with ancient architecture that are reminiscent of the great European culture. Some of the best attractions in the country include:

- Burren National Park
- The cliffs of Moher
- Killarney National Park
- The Book of Kells
- Kilmainham Gaol Museum
- The Ring of Kerry
- Glendalough
- Powerscourt House and Gardens
- The Little Museum of Dublin
- The Rock of Cashel
- Blarney Castle and The Blarney Stone
- Kinsale

My last visit to Ireland had lent me several memorable sights and an unforgettable experience of getting to know the Irish food, the people and the culture. The whole atmosphere is binding your mind and soul into it; and you feel like getting lost in the streets of Dublin and Connemara. If you haven't been to Ireland yet, then try its authentic meals and lovely recipes from the cookbook to spread the traditional Irish aromas all around you.

Breakfast

Corned Beef Hash and Eggs

Preparation time: 15 minutes
Cook time: 33 minutes
Nutrition facts (per serving): 328 Cal (17g fat, 21g protein, 8g fiber)

This corned beef hash and egg make an energizing breakfast, loaded with lots of proteins and fibers.

Ingredients (6 servings)

3 tablespoon olive oil
1 onion, chopped
1 bell pepper, chopped
3 large russet potatoes, cubed
1 teaspoon dried oregano
Salt, to taste
Black pepper, to taste
1 cup chopped corned beef
6 large eggs

Preparation

At 400 degrees F preheat your oven. Sauté the onion and the bell pepper with oil in a suitable skillet for 5 minutes. Stir in the black pepper, salt, oregano and potatoes. Cook for 20 minutes. Add the corned beef and sauté for 5 minutes. Make 6 wells in the mixture and crack one egg in each well. Drizzle with black pepper and salt on top, and then bake for 8 minutes. Serve warm.

Irish Potato Pancake (Boxty)

Preparation time: 15 minutes
Cook time: 30 minutes
Nutrition facts (per serving): 286 Cal (11g fat, 2g protein, 3g fiber)

This potato pancake is a must-have for every breakfast or snack table. Accordingly, with the help of this recipe, you can cook them in no time.

Ingredients (4 servings)
4 large Yukon Gold potatoes, peeled
¾ cup whole milk
1 ¼ teaspoon fine salt
1 large egg
⅓ cup all-purpose flour
¼ teaspoon black pepper
2 tablespoon unsalted butter, cubed

Preparation
Add the potatoes, water, and a pinch of salt to a cooking pot and boil them for 15 minutes until soft. Drain and mash the potatoes in a bowl. Stir in milk, salt, egg, and flour and mix evenly. Set a skillet, greased with butter and let it heat. Add ¼ cup potato batter and spread into ¼ inch thick round. Cook for 5 minutes per side and then cook more pancakes. Serve.

White Pudding with Oatmeal

Preparation time: 15 minutes
Cook time: 30 minutes
Nutrition facts (per serving): 256 Cal (5.2g fat, 23g protein, 18g fiber)

Have you tried the famous white pudding for breakfast? Well, here's an Irish delight that adds oatmeal to your morning meal in a delicious way.

Ingredients (4 servings)
1 lb. beef suet, ground
1 ¼ lb. oatmeal
3 ½ teaspoon salt
1 teaspoon white pepper
¼ cup cold water
2 tablespoon ½ onion, chopped
½ leeks, chopped
1 egg

Preparation
Soak the oatmeal in milk in a bowl, overnight and then drain. Mix the oatmeal with egg, suet, and the rest of the ingredients in a large bowl. Stuff the oatmeal mixture in the hot dog casings and tie them. Add the tied sausage to hot water in a cooking pot and cook for 30 minutes. Drain and serve.

Irish Scones

Preparation time: 15 minutes
Cook time: 35 minutes
Nutrition facts (per serving): 213 Cal (20g fat, 2g protein, 7g fiber)

The Irish scones are famous for their delicious flavor and fluffy texture. Made from egg and lots of dairy, these scones pair well with all the jams.

Ingredients (8 servings)
3 ½ cups all-purpose flour
5 teaspoon baking powder
1 generous pinch of salt
¼ cup sugar
¼ cup salted butter cold, cubed
1 egg
¼ cup double cream
¾ cup whole milk
Milk, to glaze

Preparation
Mix all the dry ingredients with cold butter in a bowl to make a coarse mixture. Beat the egg with milk and the rest of the liquid ingredients and then mix well until smooth. Fold in chocolate chips, citrus rind, berries, and raisins. Next, mix evenly. Divide the prepared dough into 12- 1-inch thick scones using cutters. Place the scones on a baking tray greased with cooking spray. Drizzle milk to glaze and bake for 35 minutes at 350 degrees F. Serve.

Irish Soda Bread

Preparation time: 10 minutes
Cook time: 46 minutes
Nutrition facts (per serving): 378 Cal (16g fat, 4g protein, 2g fiber)

This Irish soda bread tastes heavenly when cooked and baked at home. Serve warm with your favorite breakfast meal on the side.

Ingredients (6 servings)
1 ¾ cups buttermilk
1 large egg
4 ¼ cups all-purpose flour
3 tablespoon granulated sugar
1 teaspoon baking soda
1 teaspoon salt
5 tablespoon unsalted butter, cubed
1 cup raisins

Preparation
At 400 degrees F, preheat your oven. Layer an 8 inch round baking pan with parchment paper. Mix all the dry ingredients in a suitable mixing bowl. Then cut in the butter and mix until crumbly. Stir in the liquid ingredients and mix until smooth. Fold in the raisins and knead the prepared dough for 30 seconds. Spread the prepared dough in the pan and bake for 45 minutes. Allow it to cool and then slice. Serve.

Irish Oatmeal

Preparation time: 15 minutes
Cook time: 30 minutes
Nutrition facts (per serving): 256 Cal (16g fat, 11g protein, 6g fiber)

Irish oatmeal is another nutritious yet simple meal for the breakfast table. It has lots of nutrients and fibers to the table, along with healthy ingredients, that are cooked in a tempting combination.

Ingredients (4 servings)

4 cups water
1 teaspoon salt
1 cup steel-cut oats
4 teaspoon brown sugar

Preparation

Add water and salt to a suitable cooking pot and cook to a boil. Stir in the oats and reduce their heat. Cook on a simmer for almost 30 minutes with occasional stirring. Divide the oatmeal into the four-serving bowls. Drizzle brown sugar on top and serve.

Irish Quiche

Preparation time: 15 minutes
Cook time: 70 minutes
Nutrition facts (per serving): 410 Cal (6g fat, 20g protein, 1.4g fiber)

Try this Irish quiche for your breakfast, and you'll forget about the rest. The recipe is simple and gives you lots of nutrients in one place.

Ingredients (6 servings)

Crust

1 ¾ cups all-purpose flour

1 teaspoon salt

½ teaspoon granulated sugar

½ teaspoon dried dill

12 tablespoon Irish butter, cubed

5 tablespoon cold beer

Filling

6 whole eggs

¼ teaspoon salt

¼ teaspoon black pepper

1 teaspoon dried dill

¾ cup milk

12 maple breakfast sausage links, cooked and chopped

3 slices provolone cheese

¼ cup Colby cheese, chopped

Preparation

At 400 degrees F, preheat your oven. Mix the flour with dill, sugar, and salt in a large mixing bowl. Cut in the butter and mix until crumbly. Stir in the cold beer and mix until smooth. Knead the prepared dough over a floured surface and spread this dough on a 9-inch pie plate. Bake the pie crust for almost 10 minutes in the preheated oven. Then reduce the oven's heat to 325 degrees F. Beat the eggs with dill, black pepper, salt and milk in a small bowl. Spread half of the sausage and half of the egg's mixture in the baked crust and top them with the cheese. Add the remaining sausage and the egg mixture. Bake this sausage pie for 60 minutes in the oven. Slice and serve.

Irish Tea Scones

Preparation time: 10 minutes
Cook time: 10 minutes
Nutrition facts (per serving): 291 Cal (33g fat, 9g protein, 2g fiber)

These Irish Tea Scones are known as the classic Irish breakfast, a good version of the basic scones. Plus, they're super simple to make.

Ingredients (6 servings)

1 ¾ cups flour

¼ cup granulated sugar

2 teaspoon baking powder

½ teaspoon salt

4 tablespoon Irish butter

⅓ cup raisins

½ cup milk

1 beaten egg

Preparation

Mix the flour with sugar, baking powder, salt, and Irish butter in a bowl until crumbly. Stir in the egg and milk, and then mix evenly. Fold in the raisons and mix evenly. Divide the prepared dough into 12 scones using a cookie cutter. Place the scones on a baking sheet lined with parchment paper. Bake the scones for 10 minutes in the oven at 350 degrees F. Serve.

Irish Cheddar Scones

Preparation time: 15 minutes

Cook time: 17 minutes

Nutrition facts (per serving): 226 Cal (24g fat, 4g protein, 1g fiber)

The famous cheddar scones are one of the Irish specialties, and everyone must try this interesting combination of different toppings.

Ingredients (6 servings)

2 ½ cups all-purpose flour

1 teaspoon baking powder

½ teaspoon baking soda

½ teaspoon salt

½ cup butter, cold, cubed

1 cup Cheddar cheese, shredded

8 bacon slices, cooked

¾ cups buttermilk

1 egg, lightly beaten

1 tablespoon chives, chopped

3 tablespoon buttermilk

Preparation

Mix the flour, salt, baking soda, and baking powder in a suitable bowl. Cut in the butter and mix until crumbly. Stir in the chives, bacon, and shredded cheese and then mix well. Add the egg and buttermilk and, then mix until smooth. Knead this dough on a floured surface, divide the prepared dough into 8 scones in a baking sheet, lined with wax paper, cover, and refrigerate for 10 minutes.

Brush the scones with buttermilk and bake for 17 minutes at 375 degrees F. Allow them to cool and serve.

Irish Soda Furls

Preparation time: 15 minutes
Cook time: 12 minutes
Nutrition facts (per serving): 211 Cal (17g fat, 6g protein, 0.7g fiber)

These soda furls are the best way to enjoy soft and savory bread in the morning in the Irish style. Serve with freshly cooked eggs.

Ingredients (4 servings)
2 cups all-purpose flour
1 teaspoon baking soda
½ teaspoon salt
1 cup buttermilk
Oil, for greasing
Butter and jam, for serving

Preparation
Mix baking soda, salt, flour in a large bowl. Stir in the buttermilk and then mix evenly. Spread this dough into ¾ inch thick sheet and cut into four quadrants using a pizza cutter. Set a suitable skillet over medium heat and grease it with oil. Sear the prepared dough portions for 6 minutes per side. Serve warm with jam and butter on top.

Irish Cream Oatmeal

Preparation time: 10 minutes
Cook time: 5 minutes
Nutrition facts (per serving): 217 Cal (14g fat, 9g protein, 0.3g fiber)

This cream oatmeal is a perfect morning meal! Keep it ready in the refrigerator to serve with your favorite jam. It's super-rich, healthy, and delicious.

Ingredients (2 servings)

½ cup old-fashioned rolled oats
1 teaspoon brown sugar
1 pinch salt
1 pinch cinnamon
¾ cup water
3 tablespoon Irish cream
1 teaspoon cacao nibs
Sprinkles

Preparation

Mix oats, water, cinnamon, salt, and brown sugar in a suitable saucepan. Next, cover and cook for 5 minutes on a simmer. Garnish with cream, cacao nibs, and sprinkles. Serve.

Irish Buttermilk Pancakes

Preparation time: 15 minutes

Cook time: 16 minutes

Nutrition facts (per serving): 242 Cal (8g fat, 2g protein, 1g fiber)

If you haven't tried the Irish buttermilk pancakes before, then here comes a simple and easy to cook recipe that you can prepare at home in no time with minimum efforts.

Ingredients (4 servings)

2 cups plain flour

4 tablespoon sugar

1 ½ teaspoon bicarbonate of soda

1 egg

2 ½ cups buttermilk

Preparation

Blend the flour with sugar, soda, eggs, and buttermilk in a mixer. Set a suitable frying pan over medium heat and grease it with cooking spray. Pour a ladle of the batter into the hot pan and cook for 2 minutes per side. Cook more pancakes in the same way. Serve.

Irish Oatmeal Brulee

Preparation time: 5 minutes
Cook time: 37 minutes
Nutrition facts (per serving): 231 Cal (20g fat, 2g protein, 6g fiber)

Irish Oatmeal Brulee is one of the most delicious breakfast meals to try. Modify with different variations for its toppings as well.

Ingredients (8 servings)

8 cups milk

2 cups steel-cut oat

1 (3 inches) cinnamon stick

1 orange peel

1 dash salt

¾ cup dried cranberries

½ cup golden raisins

½ cup maple syrup

Buttermilk, if desired

½ cup packed brown sugar

Preparation

Mix oats, salt, orange peel, cinnamon and milk in a cooking pan and cook to a boil. Reduce its heat, cover, and cook on a simmer for 30 minutes until it thickens. Allow it to cool and then discard the orange peel and cinnamon. Stir in syrup, raisins, and cranberries, cover, and leave for 2 minutes. Divide the oatmeal into 8 (6oz.) ramekins and place them on a baking sheet. Drizzle brown sugar on top and broil for 7 minutes until caramelized. Serve.

Appetizers and Snacks

Irish Potato Bites

Preparation time: 15 minutes
Cook time: 35 minutes
Nutrition facts (per serving): 230 Cal (22g fat, 10g protein, 1.4g fiber)

If you haven't tried the Irish potato bites before, then here comes a simple and easy to cook recipe that you can easily prepare and cook at home in no time with minimum efforts.

Ingredients (20 servings)

20 red potatoes, small
½ cup corned beef
¼ cup cheddar cheese, shredded
1 tablespoon butter, melted
⅛ teaspoon salt
Sour cream, to serve

Preparation

Add the potatoes and water to a suitable pan and cook until the potatoes are soft. Drain and allow them to cool. Cut the small potatoes in half and scoop out some flesh from the center, and then transfer to a bowl. Stir in the butter, corned beef, and cheese, and then mix well. Adjust the seasoning with salt and divide this mixture into the potato halves. Place the potato halves in the baking sheet and bake for 10 minutes. Garnish with sour cream and serve.

Shrimp and Cucumber Bites

Preparation time: 10 minutes
Nutrition facts (per serving): 162 Cal (13g fat, 15g protein, 2g fiber)

If you can't think of anything to cook and make in a short time, then try these shrimp and cucumber bites because they have great taste and wonderful texture to serve at the table.

Ingredients (4 servings)

2 English cucumbers

½ cup garlic herb creamed cheese

30 shrimp, peeled, deveined and cooked

Salt and black pepper, to taste

Preparation

Pat dry the shrimp and season them with black pepper and salt. Peel and slice the cucumbers, then pat them dry. Add a teaspoon of cream cheese mixture on top of all of the cucumber slices and place a shrimp on the top. Serve.

Irish Pub Cheese

Preparation time: 15 minutes
Nutrition facts (per serving): 206 Cal (29g fat, 4g protein, 0.1g fiber)

The appetizing pub cheese makes a great addition to the menu, and it looks great when served at the table.

Ingredients (8 servings)
14 oz. Irish cheddar
4 oz. cream cheese
½ cup light Irish-style beer
1 garlic clove
1 ½ teaspoon ground mustard
1 teaspoon paprika

Preparation
Blend cheddar cheese with cream cheese, beer, garlic, mustard, and paprika in a blender until smooth. Serve.

Irish Guacamole

Preparation time: 15 minutes
Nutrition facts (per serving): 279 Cal (5.2g fat, 2.8g protein, 3g fiber)

If you haven't tried the Irish Guacamole, then you must now as it has no parallel in taste and texture.

Ingredients (6 servings)

1 large potato, cubed and boiled

2 large avocados

1 jalapeño, diced

2 tablespoon unsalted butter

¼ cup sour cream

2 tablespoon cilantro

½ lime, juice only

1 pinch salt and black pepper

½ cup salsa

Preparation

Mash the potatoes with avocados in a bowl, add jalapenos, sour cream, butter, cilantro, lime juice, black pepper, salt, and salsa, and then mix well. Serve.

Irish Spuds and Dip

Preparation time: 10 minutes
Cook time: 30 minutes
Nutrition facts (per serving): 231 Cal (9.5g fat, 9.7g protein, 9g fiber)

Who doesn't like to eat potatoes? Spud lovers, get ready to enjoy a heart-melting potato appetizer and green dip on this menu.

Ingredients (12 servings)

2 lbs. baking potatoes

2 tablespoon olive oil

1 teaspoon chili powder

1 teaspoon salt

1 cup ranch dressing

¼ teaspoon green food color

Preparation

At 450 degrees F, preheat your oven. Cut the potatoes into wedges and toss them with oil, salt, and chili powder in a large bowl. Spread them in a baking sheet lined with a foil sheet. Bake them for 30 minutes. Mix ranch dressing with food color in a bowl and serve the potatoes with this dip. Enjoy.

Reuben Dip

Preparation time: 15 minutes
Cook time: 20 minutes
Nutrition facts (per serving): 232 Cal (11g fat, 23g protein, 3g fiber)

This dip will satisfy your cream cheese cravings in no time. It's quick to make if you have corned beef and sauerkraut at home.

Ingredients (6 servings)

1 (8 oz.) package cream cheese, softened

½ cup Thousand Island dressing

8 oz. corned beef chopped

1 cup sauerkraut, drained and squeezed

2 cups Swiss cheese, shredded

Preparation

Mix cream cheese with island dressing, corned beef, sauerkraut, and Swiss cheese in a baking dish. Bake for about 20 minutes at 400 degrees F. Serve.

Irish Cheese Dip

Preparation time: 15 minutes
Cook time: 40 minutes
Nutrition facts (per serving): 246 Cal (23g fat, 12g protein, 3g fiber)

Irish cheese dip is another Irish-inspired delight that you should definitely try on this cuisine. Serve with the flavorsome chips.

Ingredients (12 servings)

1 (8 oz.) large package of cream cheese

1 small onion, sliced

1 tablespoon of butter

2 tablespoons of beer

Pinch of sugar

1 cup of cheddar cheese, shredded

1 teaspoon of honey

1 ½ teaspoon of brown mustard

1 teaspoon of dried thyme

2 tablespoons of Jameson Irish Whiskey

Salt and black pepper, to taste

Cayenne pepper, to taste

Preparation

Sauté the onion with sugar, butter, and beer in a suitable pan for 15 minutes over medium heat. Meanwhile, mix the cream cheese with beer, shredded cheddar, thyme, mustard, and honey in a bowl. Add the whiskey to the same pan and deglaze it. Pour this whiskey into the cream cheese mixture and then mix well. Add black pepper and salt for seasoning. Add this mixture to a ramekin and bake for 25 minutes at 350 degrees F. Garnish with cayenne pepper. Serve.

Cheesy Reuben Appetizer

Preparation time: 10 minutes
Cook time: 15 minutes
Nutrition facts (per serving): 301 Cal (3g fat, 4g protein, 4g fiber)

What about this deliciously cheesy appetizer? If you haven't tried it before, now is the time to cook this delicious mix at home using simple and healthy ingredients.

Ingredients (6 servings)

1 package (8 oz.) cream cheese, softened

1 ½ cups Swiss cheese, shredded

½ cup Thousand Island dressing

4 oz. deli-sliced corned beef, chopped

½ cup well-drained sauerkraut

Pretzel crackers, to serve

Cocktail rye bread slices, to serve

Chopped fresh chives, to serve

Sliced radishes, to serve

Preparation

At 400 degrees F, preheat your oven. Mix cream cheese with corned beef, dressing, and 1 cup Swiss cheese in a suitable bowl. Spread this mixture on a pie plate, top it with sauerkraut, and add the remaining ½ cup Swiss cheese. Cover and refrigerate this cheese mixture for 24 hours. Bake this appetizer for 15 minutes. Serve.

Irish Potato Bites

Preparation time: 10 minutes

Cook time: 45 minutes

Nutrition facts (per serving): 227 Cal (15g fat, 11g protein, 2.1g fiber)

Irish potato bites are the best appetizers to find in Irish cuisine. They're loaded with nutrients as prepared with potatoes, cheese, and cream.

Ingredients (6 servings)

3 tablespoon unsalted butter, melted

⅓ cup heavy cream

½ teaspoon salt

⅛ teaspoon black pepper

1 garlic clove, minced

2 lbs. russet potatoes, peeled and sliced

¾ cup Dubliner cheese, shredded

Preparation

At 375 degrees F, preheat your oven. Grease a muffin pan with cooking spray. Mix garlic with melted butter, black pepper, salt, and heavy cream in a small bowl. Cut each potato slice evenly into a 2-inch round using a biscuit cutter. Place five potato slices in each muffin pan and top them with cream mixture and shredded cheese. Cover this muffin pan with a foil sheet and bake for 25 minutes at 375 degrees F. Uncover and bake for 20 minutes. Allow them to cool and serve.

Guinness Dubliner Dip

Preparation time: 15 minutes
Cook time: 65 minutes
Nutrition facts (per serving): 146 Cal (21g fat, 9g protein, 4.1g fiber)

Guinness Dubliner Dip is everyone's favorite go-to meal when it comes to serving Irish meals; you can prepare it in no time.

Ingredients (8 servings)

1 rye bread loaf, sliced

Olive oil

Salt, to taste

Dip

2 tablespoon unsalted butter

1 yellow onion, sliced

Salt, to taste

1 (8 oz.) brick, cream cheese

7 oz. Dubliner cheese, grated

¼ cup mayonnaise

¼ cup Guinness beer

Preparation

At 400 degrees F, preheat your oven. Spread the bread on a baking sheet. Brush the bread with oil and drizzle salt on top. Bake the bread for 12 minutes and flip once cooked halfway through. Cut the toast in half. Sauté the onions with butter and a pinch of salt in a suitable skillet for 25 minutes until caramelized. Mix the cream cheese with caramelized onions, cheese, and mayonnaise in a bowl. Stir in Guinness beer and the rest of the ingredients, and then mix evenly. Spread this mixture in a baking and drizzle cheese on top and then bake for 28 minutes. Allow the dip to cool and serve.

Irish Mashed Potatoes (Colcannon)

Preparation time: 10 minutes
Cook time: 20 minutes
Nutrition facts (per serving): 172 Cal (5g fat, 1.4g protein, 2g fiber)

Irish mashed potatoes are another great side serving for the table, and you can serve them a delicious and healthy snack meal as well.

Ingredients (8 servings)

1 lb. red potatoes washed

4 tablespoon unsalted butter

½ cup whole milk

2 tablespoon olive oil

1 large onion sliced

6 cups cabbage, shredded

1 teaspoon salt

¼ teaspoon black pepper

⅓ cup chives, chopped

1 package cooked buffalo ranch

Preparation

Boil the potatoes in water in a cooking pot until soft and then drain. Sauté the onion with olive oil in a cooking pot until golden brown. Stir in the shredded cabbage, black pepper, and salt. Next, mix well. Mash the boiled potatoes in a suitable bowl, add milk and butter, and then mix evenly. Stir in the cabbage mixture, onion, and chives. Mix and serve.

Irish Nachos Potatoes

Preparation time: 10 minutes
Cook time: 40 minutes
Nutrition facts (per serving): 256 Cal (1.5g fat, 7g protein, 2g fiber)

Here's another most popular snack in Irish cuisine, and it has this great taste that it takes from the mix of cheese and jalapenos.

Ingredients (6 servings)

1 ½ lbs. russet potatoes, sliced

2 tablespoon olive oil

Salt and black pepper to taste

1 cup cheese, shredded

1 package bacon cooked and chopped

2 scallions sliced

1 teaspoon cilantro

Dip

4 oz. sour cream

1 tomato diced

½ cup jalapeño peppers sliced

Preparation

At 450 degrees F, preheat your oven. Toss the sliced potatoes with oil on a baking sheet and bake for 15 minutes. Flip and bake for another 20 minutes. Spread the potatoes in a skillet, drizzle cheese, black pepper, salt and bacon, and then bake for 5 minutes. Garnish with cilantro and scallions. Serve.

Salads

Irish Pub Salad

Preparation time: 10 minutes
Nutrition facts (per serving): 211 Cal (20g fat, 4g protein, 13g fiber)

This salad is the right fit to serve with all your Irish entrees. Here the lettuce and green beans are mixed with other veggies to make an amazing combination.

Ingredients (4 servings)
Dressing
½ cup mayonnaise
2 tablespoon rice vinegar
1 teaspoon dried tarragon
1 tablespoon Dijon mustard
3 teaspoon water

Salad
8 cups torn Boston lettuce
1 cup pickled beets
1 cup pickled green beans
½ cup cucumber, sliced
1 cup tomatoes, halved
1 cup chopped celery
½ cup cabbage, shredded
1 cup onions, sliced
4 hard-boiled eggs, peeled, sliced
4 oz. cheddar cheese

Preparation

Mix all the pub salad dressing ingredients in a salad bowl. Spread the rest of the ingredients on a salad platter and pour the dressing on top. Serve.

Irish Orange Spinach Salad

Preparation time: 10 minutes
Nutrition facts (per serving): 253 Cal (2g fat, 1g protein, 4g fiber)

This orange spinach salad is a delicious and healthy salad, which has a refreshing taste due to the use of herbs and spices in it. It's great to serve with skewers.

Ingredients (4 servings)
Salad
2 oranges, cut into slices

1 pear, sliced

½ cup feta cheese

¼ cup roasted pistachios, chopped

¼ cup fresh basil, chopped

4 heaping handfuls of spinach

Dressing
3 tablespoon olive oil

1 ⅓ tablespoon orange juice

1 teaspoon honey

1 teaspoon apple cider vinegar

1 tablespoon lime juice

Salt to taste

Preparation
Mix all the spinach salad dressing ingredients in a salad bowl. Toss in the rest of the orange salad ingredients and then serve.

Irish Cheese Salad

Preparation time: 10 minutes

Nutrition facts (per serving): 179 Cal (16g fat, 15g protein, 3g fiber)

The Irish cheese salad is a special fresh veggie salad, and it's excellent to serve with all the different entrees. Use this quick and simple recipe to get it ready in no time.

Ingredients (6 servings)

3 leaves butter lettuce

1 hardboiled egg

3 slices deli ham

1 medium tomato vine-ripened

¼ cup cheddar cheese grated

1 tablespoon mayonnaise

6 slices English cucumber peeled

2 tablespoon coleslaw

2 tablespoon cottage cheese

2 tablespoon carrot

2 tablespoon green onions chopped

Preparation

Toss all the Irish salad ingredients in a salad bowl. Serve.

Broccoli, Feta and Tomato Salad

Preparation time: 10 minutes
Nutrition facts (per serving): 276 Cal (17g fat, 7g protein, 3g fiber)

It's as if the Irish menu is incomplete without this broccoli tomato salad. Made from broccoli, feta, and tomatoes, these ingredients offer lots of nutritional value to this salad.

Ingredients (6 servings)
Salad
3 ½ oz. walnuts, chopped
14 oz. broccoli, chopped into florets
8 oz. cherry tomatoes, halved
3 ½ oz. Feta cheese, chopped

Dressing
¼ cup rapeseed oil
3 tablespoon wine vinegar
2 garlic cloves, crushed
2 teaspoon Dijon mustard
1 teaspoon dried oregano
Salt and black pepper, to taste

Preparation
Mix all the broccoli salad dressing ingredients in a salad bowl. Toss in the rest of the broccoli salad ingredients and then mix well.

Strawberry Spinach Salad

Preparation time: 10 minutes
Cook time: 10 minutes
Nutrition facts (per serving): 155 Cal (8g fat, 3g protein, 2g fiber)

If you haven't tried the strawberry spinach salad before, then here comes a simple and easy to cook recipe that you can recreate at home in no time with minimum efforts.

Ingredients (6 servings)
Salad
10 ½ oz. fresh spinach
14 oz. strawberries, de-stemmed and quartered
4 scallions, sliced
3 ½ oz. goat's cheese, crumbled

Croutons
3 ½ oz. leftover bread, cut into cubes
2 tablespoon rapeseed oil
2 teaspoon dried basil
Salt and black pepper, to taste

Dressing
4 tablespoon balsamic vinegar
3 tablespoon rapeseed oil
1½ tablespoon poppy seeds
1½ tablespoon honey
½ teaspoon Dijon mustard
Salt and black pepper, to taste

Preparation

Toss the bread cubes with oil, black pepper, salt and basil in baking, then bake until golden and crispy. Mix all the spinach salad dressing ingredients in a salad bowl. Toss in the croutons and the rest of the ingredients and then serve.

Carrot and Pumpkin Seed Salad

Preparation time: 10 minutes
Nutrition facts (per serving): 243 Cal (13g fat, 5g protein, 2g fiber)

Irish carrot and pumpkin seed salad is iconic for everyone to cook on this menu. It's made of carrots, raisins, and herbs.

Ingredients (6 servings)
Salad
4 medium carrots, grated
2 tablespoon raisins
4 tablespoon pumpkin seeds, roasted
8 radishes, sliced
3 tablespoon mixed fresh herbs, chopped
8 oz. rocket or arugula

Dressing
1 tablespoon rapeseed oil
1 tablespoon apple cider vinegar
1 teaspoon honey
½ teaspoon Dijon mustard
Salt and black pepper, to taste

Preparation
Mix all the carrot salad dressing ingredients in a salad bowl. Toss in the rest of the ingredients. Serve.

Mango, Cucumber and Bean Salad

Preparation time: 15 minutes
Nutrition facts (per serving): 381 Cal (5g fat, 3g protein, 6g fiber)

If you haven't tried the mango and bean salad before, then here comes a simple and easy to cook recipe that you can recreate at home in no time with minimum efforts.

Ingredients (6 servings)

1 mango, peeled, diced

½ cucumber, cut in half lengthways, seeds removed and sliced

14 oz. tin of kidney beans drained and rinsed

2 scallions, sliced

1 handful of coriander leaves

Juice and zest of ½ lime

1 tablespoon olive oil

Preparation

Mix the beans with mango and the rest of the ingredients in a salad bowl. Serve.

Irish Watercress Salad

Preparation time: 15 minutes
Cook time: 60 minutes
Nutrition facts (per serving): 252 Cal (13g fat, 24g protein, 4g fiber)

The Irish watercress salad is a delight to serve with all entrees. It's known for its comforting effects, and the meal offers a very energizing combination of ingredients.

Ingredients (6 servings)

2 medium beets
2 small heads of Bibb lettuce
2 bunches watercress
2 tablespoon crème fraiche
1 tablespoon parsley, chopped
5 tablespoon olive oil
3 tablespoon herb-infused white vinegar
Salt and black pepper, to taste
1 dozen quail eggs, boiled, peeled and diced
½ cup chervil leaves, chopped

Preparation

Add the beets to a cooking pot filled with water, cover and cook on a simmer for 1 hour. Drain and allow the beetroots to cool. Peel and cut them into julienne. Separate the lettuce leaves. Remove the watercress stems. Mix the crème fraiche with the rest of the dressing ingredients in a salad bowl. Spread the lettuce on the serving platter. Top the leaves with eggs, watercress, and beets. Pour the prepared dressing on top. Serve.

Irish Green Salad

Preparation time: 10 minutes
Nutrition facts (per serving): 260 Cal (3g fat, 3g protein, 11g fiber)

Try this Irish green salad with your favorite herbs on top. Adding a dollop of cream or yogurt will make it even richer in taste.

Ingredients (6 servings)

6 cups mixed greens

1 medium apple, unpeeled, diced

16 asparagus spears

2 tablespoon mint, minced

2 oz. Irish cheddar cheese, cubed

1 small parsnip, peeled and grated

2 large green bell pepper

3 tablespoon raisins

Dressing

½ cup whole milk buttermilk

cream, for thinning

3 tablespoon apple cider vinegar

2 tablespoon sour cream

Salt, to taste

Black pepper, to taste

Preparation

Mix all the green salad dressing ingredients in a salad bowl. Toss in the rest of the ingredients. Serve.

Soups

Irish Leek and Potato Soup

Preparation time: 10 minutes
Cook time: 23 minutes
Nutrition facts (per serving): 361 Cal (14g fat, 2g protein, 2g fiber)

Enjoy this Irish leek and potato soup recipe with mixed potatoes flavors. Adding cream or sour cream on top creates a very strong taste to the soup.

Ingredients (4 servings)

4 tablespoon butter

1 onion chopped

3 leeks trimmed, sliced, the rinsed, and dried

2 russet potatoes peeled and diced

3 ½ cups chicken stock

½ cup frozen peas

Salt and black pepper, to taste

Garnish

Sour cream

Snipped chives

Preparation

Sauté the onions, potato, and leeks with butter in a large pot for 5 minutes. Stir in stock, cover and cook on a simmer for 15 minutes. Add the peas, black pepper, and salt. Cook for 3 minutes and then garnish with chives and sour cream. Serve warm.

Irish Potato Soup

Preparation time: 10 minutes
Cook time: 65 minutes
Nutrition facts (per serving): 210 Cal (11g fat, 2g protein, 6g fiber)

Make this Irish basic potatoes soup in no time and enjoy it with some garnish on top. Adding a drizzle of paprika on top makes it super tasty.

Ingredients (6 servings)

½ cup unsalted butter

1 medium onion, sliced

3 baking potatoes, peeled and sliced

3 (14 ½-oz.) cans chicken broth

1 teaspoon salt

¼ teaspoon black pepper

Toppings

Cheddar cheese, shredded

Crumbled cooked bacon

Chopped fresh chives

Preparation

Sauté the onion with butter in a large saucepan, cover, and cook for 20 minutes. Stir in potatoes, cover, and cook for 15 minutes. Add the broth and the rest of the soup ingredients; then cook for 30 minutes on a simmer. Puree the soup in a blender. Garnish with toppings and serve warm.

Fennel Carrot Soup

Preparation time: 15 minutes
Cook time: 50 minutes
Nutrition facts (per serving): 117 Cal (2g fat, 3 protein, 2g fiber)

Fennel carrot soup is also quite famous in the region; in fact, and it's essential to try because of its high nutritional content.

Ingredients (6 servings)

1 tablespoon butter
½ teaspoon fennel seed
1 ½ lbs. carrots, sliced
1 medium sweet potato, peeled and cubed
1 medium apple, peeled and cubed
3 cans (14 ½ oz.) vegetable broth
2 tablespoon uncooked long-grain rice
1 bay leaf
¼ teaspoon curry powder
1 tablespoon lemon juice
½ teaspoon salt
¼ teaspoon white pepper
2 tablespoon fresh parsley, minced

Preparation

Sauté the fennel with butter in a suitable pan for 3 minutes. Stir in the apple, sweet potatoes, and carrots and then cook for 5 minutes. Add the curry powder, bay leaf, rice and broth. Next, cook to a boil. Reduce it heat, cover and cook for 30 minutes. Discard the bay leaf and puree the soup until smooth. Stir in black pepper, salt, and lemon juice. Cover and cook for 5 minutes. Garnish with parsley. Serve warm.

Mushroom and Barley Soup

Preparation time: 10 minutes
Cook time: 8 hours
Nutrition facts (per serving): 180 Cal (4g fat, 15g protein, 3g fiber)

This mushroom and barley soup is everything I was looking for. The barley, spices, and mushrooms make a complete package for a health enthusiast like me.

Ingredients (6 servings)

1 lb. baby Portobello mushrooms, sliced
3 medium carrots, chopped
3 celery ribs, chopped
1 medium onion, chopped
1 cup medium pearl barley
1 teaspoon dried thyme
1 teaspoon black pepper
5 cups water
4 cups beef stock
3 teaspoon salt
1 large egg, lightly beaten
1 lb. ground turkey

Preparation

Add the mushrooms, carrots, ribs, onion, barley, 2 ½ teaspoon salt, thyme, black pepper, water, and stock to a slow cooker. Mix the egg with the remaining salt and turkey in a bowl and make 1 ¼ inch meatballs. Add them to the soup, cover and cook on low heat for 8 hours. Serve warm.

Curried Chicken Soup

Preparation time: 15 minutes

Cook time: 36 minutes

Nutrition facts (per serving): 270 Cal (16g fat, 16g protein, 5g fiber)

You won't know until you try it! That's what people told me about this curried chicken soup, and it indeed tasted more unique and flavorsome than other chicken soups I've tried.

Ingredients (6 servings)

1 teaspoon curry powder

½ teaspoon salt

½ teaspoon black pepper

½ teaspoon cayenne pepper

1 lb. boneless chicken breasts, cubed

3 medium carrots, chopped

1 medium sweet red pepper, chopped

1 small onion, chopped

2 tablespoon olive oil

1 garlic clove, minced

1 can (15 oz.) garbanzo beans, rinsed and drained

1 can (14 ½ oz.) chicken broth

1 can (14 ½ oz.) diced tomatoes, drained

1 cup water

1 can (14 oz.) coconut milk

¾ cup fresh cilantro, minced

Preparation

Mix the chicken with cayenne, black pepper, salt, and curry in a shallow dish. Cook the chicken with onion, red pepper, and carrots with oil in a suitable skillet for 4 minutes. Stir in the garlic and sauté for 2 minutes. Stir in the water, tomatoes, broth, and beans and then boil. Cover and cook for 30 minutes on a simmer. Add the coconut milk and garnish with cilantro. Serve warm.

Creamy Root Veggie Soup

Preparation time: 15 minutes

Cook time: 55 minutes

Nutrition facts (per serving): 295 Cal (17g fat, 8g protein, 3g fiber)

If you haven't tried the root veggie soup before, then here comes a simple and easy cook this recipe that you can recreate at home in no time with minimum efforts.

Ingredients (6 servings)

4 bacon strips, chopped

1 large onion, chopped

3 garlic cloves, minced

1 large celery root, peeled and cubed

6 medium parsnips, peeled and cubed

6 cups chicken stock

1 bay leaf

1 cup heavy whipping cream

2 teaspoon minced fresh thyme

1 teaspoon salt

¼ teaspoon white pepper

¼ teaspoon ground nutmeg

Minced fresh thyme

Preparation

Sauté the bacon in a Dutch oven until crispy then transfer to a plate. Add the onion to the bacon dripping and sauté for 8 minutes. Stir in the garlic and then sauté for 1 minute. Add the bay leaf, stock, parsnips, and celery root and then cook to a boil. Reduce its heat and cook for 40 minutes. Discard the bay leaf and puree the soup with an immersion blender. Add the nutmeg, black pepper, salt, thyme, and cream and then cook until warm. Garnish with bacon and thyme. Serve warm.

Beef and Vegetable Soup

Preparation time: 15 minutes

Cook time: 3 hours

Nutrition facts (per serving): 312 Cal (10g fat, 21g protein, 4g fiber)

You can give this beef and vegetable soup a try because it has a good and delicious combination of beef with carrots and peppers.

Ingredients (6 servings)

1 ½ lb. beef stew meat, diced

1 teaspoon salt

1 teaspoon seasoning blend

¾ teaspoon black pepper

2 tablespoon olive oil

4 large carrots, sliced

1 large onion, chopped

1 medium sweet red pepper, chopped

1 medium green pepper, chopped

2 garlic cloves, minced

1 cup Burgundy wine

4 cups beef broth

1 can (14 ½ oz.) diced tomatoes, undrained

2 tablespoon tomato paste

2 tablespoon Worcestershire sauce

1 bay leaf

4 medium potatoes, cubed

Preparation

Sauté the beef with oil in a suitable pan until brown then transfer to a plate. Add the remaining oil, peppers, onion and carrots to the same pan and sauté until soft. Stir in the garlic and then sauté for 1 minute. Pour in the wine to deglaze the pan. Add the bay leaf, remaining seasonings, Worcestershire sauce, tomato paste, tomatoes, broth, and beef. Next, cook to a boil, reduce its heat, and cover to cook for 2 hours. Add the potatoes and then cook for 40 minutes. Discard the bay leaf and serve warm.

Vegetable Lentil Soup

Preparation time: 15 minutes
Cook time: 50 minutes
Nutrition facts (per serving): 314 Cal (6g fat, 20g protein, 2g fiber)

This vegetable lentil soup is loved by all, young and adult. It's so simple and quick to make. This delight is great to serve at dinner tables.

Ingredients (8 servings)
6 bacon strips, chopped
1-lb. red potatoes, chopped
2 medium carrots, chopped
1 medium onion, chopped
6 garlic cloves, minced
¾ teaspoon ground cumin
½ teaspoon salt
½ teaspoon rubbed sage
½ teaspoon dried thyme
¼ teaspoon black pepper
1-½ cups dried lentils, rinsed
4 cups chicken stock

Preparation
Sauté the bacon in a suitable pan until crispy and transfer to a plate. Add the onion, potatoes, and carrots to the same pan and sauté for 8 minutes. Add the seasonings and garlic and then sauté for 1 minute. Add the stock and the lentils, boil, and reduce the heat. Finally, cook on a simmer for 35 minutes until soft. Garnish with bacon and serve warm.

Roasted Pepper Potato Soup

Preparation time: 5 minutes
Cook time: 20 minutes
Nutrition facts (per serving): 204 Cal (9g fat, 6g protein, 1.7g fiber)

Try the roasted pepper potato soup at the dinner as the soup is infused with an amazing blend of veggies and spices. Serve warm with your favorite bread.

Ingredients (6 servings)

2 medium onions, chopped

2 tablespoon canola oil

1 jar (7 oz.) roasted sweet red peppers, undrained and chopped

1 can (4 oz.) green chiles, chopped

2 teaspoon ground cumin

1 teaspoon salt

1 teaspoon ground coriander

3 cups diced peeled potatoes

3 cups vegetable broth

2 tablespoon fresh cilantro, minced

1 tablespoon lemon juice

½ cup cream cheese, cubed

Preparation

Sauté the onions with oil in a suitable saucepan until soft. Stir in the coriander, salt, cumin, chiles, and roasted peppers then cook for 2 minutes. Stir in the broth and the potatoes and then cook to a boil. Reduce its heat, cover, and cook for 15 minutes on a simmer. Add lemon juice and cilantro. Blend cream cheese with half of the soup in a blender and then pour into the pan. Serve warm.

Mulligatawny

Preparation time: 5 minutes

Cook time: 8 hours

Nutrition facts (per serving): 102 Cal (3g fat, 11g protein, 2g fiber)

This Mulligatawny soup is a typical Irish entree, which is a must to have on the Irish menu. It has this rich mix of tomato, apple, and chicken that I love.

Ingredients (6 servings)

1 can (32 oz.) chicken broth

1 can (14 ½ oz.) diced tomatoes

2 cups cooked chicken, cubed

1 large tart apple, peeled and chopped

¼ cup onion, chopped

¼ cup carrot, chopped

¼ cup green pepper, chopped

1 tablespoon fresh parsley, chopped

2 teaspoon lemon juice

1 teaspoon salt

1 teaspoon curry powder

½ teaspoon sugar

¼ teaspoon black pepper

2 whole cloves

Preparation

Add the chicken broth, tomatoes, and the rest of the ingredients to a slow cooker. Now cook for 8 hours on low heat. Discard the cloves and serve warm.

Ham and Potato-Rutabaga Chowder

Preparation time: 5 minutes
Cook time: 60 minutes
Nutrition facts (per serving): 320 Cal (32g fat, 13g protein, 0g fiber)

Simple and easy to make, this recipe is a must to try on this menu. Irish rutabaga chowder is a delight for the dinner table.

Ingredients (8 servings)

2 lbs. rutabagas, peeled and chopped
1 ¼ lbs. red potatoes, chopped
1 large onion, chopped
6 tablespoon canola oil
1 teaspoon salt
¼ teaspoon black pepper
1-½ cups cooked ham, cubed
1 medium sweet red pepper, chopped
2 celery ribs, chopped
½ cup all-purpose flour
1 ½ teaspoon onion powder
1 ½ teaspoon smoked paprika
8 cups chicken stock
1 cup heavy whipping cream
Salt and black pepper to taste

Preparation

At 425 degrees F, preheat your oven. Mix the potatoes, onion, and rutabaga in a large bowl. Stir in the black pepper, salt, and 2 tablespoon oil. Next, spread them in two 15x10 baking pans. Roast these veggies for 40 minutes in the oven. Sauté the ham with 2 tablespoon oil in a stockpot for 9 minutes. Transfer the ham to a plate. Add the remaining oil, celery, and red pepper and then sauté for 6 minutes. Add paprika, onion powder, and flour and then mix well. Pour in the stock, bring to a boil with stirring, and cook for 5 minutes until it thickens. Garnish with cream, roasted veggies, black pepper, and salt. Serve warm.

Cream of Walnut Soup

Preparation time: 5 minutes
Cook time: 35 minutes
Nutrition facts (per serving): 365 Cal (32g fat, 9g protein, 2g fiber)

Cream of walnut soup is one of the traditional Irish entrées made from walnuts, celery, and chicken broth.

Ingredients (6 servings)

3 cups chicken broth
1 cup walnuts, chopped
2 tablespoon onion, chopped
2 tablespoon celery, chopped
⅛ teaspoon ground nutmeg
2 tablespoon butter
2 tablespoon all-purpose flour
½ cup (2%) milk
1 cup half-and-half cream
Minced fresh parsley

Preparation

Boil the chicken broth with walnuts, onion, celery, and nutmeg in a cooking pot, reduce its heat, cover, and cook for 30 minutes on a simmer. Blend this mixture until smooth and then strain. Sauté the flour with butter in a suitable pan for 30 seconds and then add milk. Mix until smooth and cook for 1 minute. Stir in the walnut liquid and cream and then cook to a boil. Garnish with parsley. Serve warm.

Cabbage and Beef Soup

Preparation time: 5 minutes
Cook time: 65 minutes
Nutrition facts (per serving): 116 Cal (3g fat, 11g protein, 0.8g fiber)

A perfect mix of cabbage with beef in one soup is all that you need to expand your Irish menu. Simple and easy to make, this recipe is essential to try.

Ingredients (4 servings)
1 lb. lean ground beef
½ teaspoon garlic salt
¼ teaspoon garlic powder
¼ teaspoon black pepper
2 celery ribs, chopped
1 can (16 oz.) kidney beans, rinsed and drained
½ medium head cabbage, chopped
1 can (28 oz.) diced tomatoes, undrained
3-½ cups water
4 teaspoon beef bouillon granules
Minced fresh parsley

Preparation
Sauté the beef in a Dutch oven until brown and then add the rest of the ingredients, except the parsley. Cook this mixture to a boil, and then reduce it to heat, cover, and cook for 1 hour on a simmer. Garnish with parsley and serve warm.

Spiced Split Pea Soup

Preparation time: 15 minutes
Cook time: 10 hours 10 minutes
Nutrition facts (per serving): 139 Cal (0g fat, 8g protein, 2g fiber)

Do you want to enjoy split soup with an Irish twist? Then try this Irish split pea soup recipe. You can serve it with your favorite bread on the side.

Ingredients (4 servings)

1 cup dried green split peas
2 medium potatoes, chopped
2 medium carrots, halved and sliced
1 medium onion, chopped
1 celery rib, sliced
3 garlic cloves, minced
3 bay leaves
4 teaspoon curry powder
1 teaspoon ground cumin
½ teaspoon coarsely ground pepper
½ teaspoon ground coriander
1 can (32 oz.) chicken broth
1 can (28 oz.) diced tomatoes, undrained

Preparation

Add the potatoes, split peas, carrots, and the rest of the ingredients, except tomatoes, to a slow cooker. Cover and cook on low heat for about 10 hours. Discard the bay leaves and add the tomatoes. Mix and cook for 10 minutes. Serve warm.

Beef Barley Soup with Roasted Vegetables

Preparation time: 15 minutes
Cook time: 1 hour 50 minutes
Nutrition facts (per serving): 339 Cal (13g fat, 20g protein, 6g fiber)

The classic beef barley soup with roasted vegetables is here to complete your Irish menu. This meal can be served on all special occasions and festive celebrations.

Ingredients (8 servings)

¼ cup all-purpose flour

1 teaspoon salt

½ teaspoon black pepper

1-lb. beef stew meat, cubed

5 tablespoon olive oil

1 large Portobello mushroom, stem removed, chopped

1 medium onion, chopped

1 fennel bulb, chopped

1 garlic clove, minced

8 cups beef stock

2 cups water

2 cups peeled butternut squash, cubed

1 large baking potato, peeled and cubed

2 large carrots, cut into ½-inch slices

⅔ cup quick-cooking barley

2 teaspoon minced fresh thyme

Dash ground nutmeg

¼ cup minced fresh parsley

Preparation

Mix the beef with the flour, black pepper, and salt to coat. Set a Dutch oven with 2 tablespoon oil over medium heat. Toss in the beef and sauté until brown. Next, remove from the Dutch oven. Sauté the onion, fennel, and mushroom with 1 tablespoon oil in the same Dutch oven for 5 minutes. Stir in the garlic and sauté for 1 minute. Add the water and the stock, and then cook to a boil. Reduce its heat, cover, and cook on a simmer for 60 minutes. At 425 degrees F, preheat the oven. Toss the carrots with potato and squash with the remaining oil and roast for 25 minutes. Add these veggies, nutmeg, thyme, and barley to the soup and cook to a boil. Reduce its heat, cover, and cook on a simmer for 12 minutes. Garnish with parsley. Serve warm.

Crouton Garlic Soup

Preparation time: 15 minutes
Cook time: 80 minutes
Nutrition facts (per serving): 570 Cal (46g fat, 12g protein, 2g fiber)

The Irish crouton garlic soup is an entrée that you must serve at the winter dinner table. This recipe will add a lot of flavor, aroma, and color to your menu.

Ingredients (8 servings)
20 garlic cloves, peeled
1 tablespoon olive oil
2 large onions, halved and sliced
2 tablespoon butter
2-½ cups chicken broth
1 tablespoon fresh thyme, minced
1 bay leaf
1 cup heavy whipping cream

Croutons
2 cups sourdough bread, cubed
2 tablespoon olive oil
1 teaspoon minced fresh rosemary
¼ teaspoon salt
⅛ teaspoon black pepper

Topping
½ cup Gruyere cheese, shredded
2 tablespoon fresh parsley, minced

Preparation

Sauté the garlic with oil in a suitable skillet for 5 minutes then remove from the heat. Sauté the onions with butter in a Dutch oven until soft. Reduce its heat and cook for 30 minutes. Add the sautéed garlic, bay leaf, thyme, and broth. Cook to a boil and then reduce its heat. Cover and cook on a simmer for 20 minutes. Add the cream and discard the bay leaf. Toss the croutons with oil, black pepper, salt, and rosemary in a small bowl. Spread the bread cubes on a baking sheet and bake for 20 minutes at 400 degrees F. Add these crispy croutons on top of the soup and garnish with cheese and parsley. Serve warm.

Creamy Turnip Soup

Preparation time: 15 minutes
Cook time: 35 minutes
Nutrition facts (per serving): 138 Cal (6g fat, 4g protein, 1.2g fiber)

The Irish creamy turnip soup is here to complete your Irish menu. This meal can be served on all special occasions and memorable celebrations.

Ingredients (6 servings)

2 tablespoon butter

1 medium onion, chopped

3 garlic cloves, minced

½ cup white wine

3 lbs. turnips, peeled and cubed

1 carton (32 oz.) chicken broth

1 medium potato, peeled and cubed

1 cup half-and-half cream

½ teaspoon salt

½ teaspoon ground nutmeg

½ teaspoon olive oil

3 cups fresh baby spinach

Preparation

Sauté the onion with butter in a Dutch oven over medium-high heat until soft. Stir in the garlic and sauté for 1 minute. Add the wine and cook to a boil, then add the potatoes, broth, and turnips. Let the soup boil and then cook on a simmer for 25 minutes. Then puree the soup in a blender and return to a pan.

Add the nutmeg, salt, and cream. Sauté the spinach with oil in a skillet for 1 minute and then add to the soup. Serve warm.

Main Dishes

Traditional Irish Stew

Preparation time: 10 minutes
Cook time: 2 hours 20 minutes
Nutrition facts (per serving): 481 Cal (16g fat, 29g protein, 2g fiber)

The traditional Irish stew is here to add flavors to your dinner table, but this time with a mix of beef and potatoes. You can try it as an effortless entrée with all sorts of bread.

Ingredients (6 servings)
2 tablespoon vegetable oil
1-lb. lamb cutlets
2 lbs. potatoes, peeled and quartered
1 cup chopped carrots
1 cup chopped onion
1 cup sliced leeks, cleaned
2 tablespoon all-purpose flour
3 cups dark beef stock
3 cabbage leaves, sliced
Salt, to taste
Black pepper, to taste

Preparation
At 350 degrees F, preheat your oven. Sauté the lamb piece with 1 tablespoon oil in a cooking pot until brown. Transfer the brown meat to a Dutch oven. Top the lamb with potatoes, carrots, onion, and leeks. Add the flour to the lamb drippings in the cooking pot and then sauté for 3 minutes. Stir in 1 cup stock, mix, and cook until the mixture thickens. Pour this sauce over the lamb and

veggies. Add the remaining stock and cook for 1 hour. Stir in the cabbage, uncovered, and cook for 1 hour. Serve warm.

Irish Beef Stew

Preparation time: 10 minutes
Cook time: 2 hours 35 minutes
Nutrition facts (per serving): 401 Cal (14g fat, 29g protein, 3g fiber)

Let's have a rich and delicious combination of beef with veggies. Try it with warm bread slices, and you'll simply love it.

Ingredients (8 servings)
1 ¼ lb. chuck beef stew meat, cut into chunks
3 teaspoons of salt
¼ cup olive oil
6 large garlic cloves, minced
4 cups beef stock
2 cups water
1 cup of Guinness stout
1 cup of red wine
2 tablespoon tomato paste
1 tablespoon sugar
1 tablespoon dried thyme
1 tablespoon Worcestershire sauce
2 bay leaves
2 tablespoon butter
3 lbs. russet potatoes, peeled, cut into pieces
1 large onion, chopped
2 cups peeled carrots, chopped
½ teaspoon black pepper
2 tablespoon fresh parsley, chopped

Preparation

Sauté the beef pieces with oil in a suitable cooking pot until brown. Stir in the garlic and then sauté for 30 seconds. Stir in the bay leaves, Worcestershire sauce, thyme, sugar, tomato paste, red wine, Guinness, water, and stock and then mix well. Cook the mixture on low heat and cook for 1 hour. Sauté the onions and carrots with butter in a separate skillet for 15 minutes. Add these veggies to the stew and adjust the seasoning with black pepper and salt. Finally, cook for 40 minutes. Discard the bay leaves. Garnish with parsley. Serve warm.

Pork and Guinness Stew

Preparation time: 15 minutes
Cook time: 3 hours
Nutrition facts (per serving): 365 Cal (17g fat, 25g protein, 5.4g fiber)

It's about time to try some classic stew dish on the menu and make it more diverse and flavorsome. Serve warm with your favorite herbs on top.

Ingredients (6 servings)

2 tablespoon olive oil

2 ½ lbs. pork meat, boneless, diced

¾ teaspoon salt

¾ teaspoon black pepper

3 garlic cloves, minced

2 onions, chopped

6 oz. bacon, diced

3 tablespoon flour

15 oz. Guinness Beer

4 tablespoon tomato paste

3 cups chicken stock

3 carrots, peeled and cut into pieces

2 large celery stalks, cut into pieces

2 bay leaves

3 sprigs thyme

Preparation

Toss the pork chunks with black pepper and salt. Sauté these pork chunks with oil in a heavy pot until brown. Stir in the onion and garlic and then sauté for 3 minutes. Add the bacon and cook until crispy. Stir in the celery, carrot, and flour and then cook for 1 minute. Stir in the tomato paste, broth, thyme, bay leaves, and Guinness, cover, and cook for 2 hours on low heat. Uncover and cook for 45 minutes on a simmer. Adjust the seasoning with black pepper and salt. Lastly, remove the bay leaves and thyme. Serve.

Lamb Stew

Preparation time: 10 minutes

Cook time: 2 hours minutes

Nutrition facts (per serving): 323 Cal (13g fat, 27g protein, 1.4g fiber)

Irish lamb stew is here to make your meal special. You can always serve the stew with warm bread on the side.

Ingredients (6 servings)

4 oz. bacon strips, chopped

2 lbs. boneless leg of lamb, diced

½ tablespoon salt

1 teaspoon black pepper

¼ cup all-purpose flour

1 large yellow onion diced

4 garlic cloves minced

1 ½ cups good red wine

1 lb. button mushrooms, sliced

4 cups beef broth

1 tablespoon tomato paste

2 bay leaves

½ teaspoon dried thyme

1 ½ lbs. yellow potatoes halved

4 medium carrots, peeled and diced

¼ cup parsley chopped

Preparation

Sauté the bacon in a Dutch oven until crispy and then transfer to a plate. Spice up the lamb pieces with 1 teaspoon black pepper, ½ tablespoon salt, and ¼ cup flour in a bowl. Sauté the coated lamb in the Dutch oven until brown. Transfer the beef to the bacon. Add the onion and sauté for 2 minutes. Stir in the garlic and then sauté for 1 minute. Stir in 1 ½ cup wine to deglaze the pot. Add the sliced mushrooms and cook for almost 10 minutes. At 325 degrees F, preheat your oven. Add the lamb and bacon to the Dutch oven. Stir in the rest of the stew ingredients and then bake for 1 hr. 45 minutes in the oven. Serve warm.

Irish Duck Stew

Preparation time: 15 minutes
Cook time: 1 hour 20 minutes
Nutrition facts (per serving): 527 Cal (33g fat, 44g protein, 2g fiber)

This new version of Irish stew tastes amazing, and it's very simple and easy to cook. It's great for all duck meat lovers.

Ingredients (8 servings)
4 lbs. duck, cut into pieces
2 tablespoon vegetable oil
¼ cup all-purpose flour
2 pinches salt
Black pepper, to taste
2 pinches cayenne pepper
¼ cup vegetable oil
2 yellow onions, chopped
4 garlic cloves, crushed
¼ cup tomato paste
1 teaspoon water
3 cups Irish stout beer
2 sprigs of fresh thyme
4 large potatoes, chopped
2 cups carrot, chopped
2 tablespoon parsley, chopped

Preparation

Toss the duck with black pepper and salt. Sauté them with oil in a heavy pot until brown. Stir in the onion and the garlic and then sauté for 3 minutes. Stir in the carrot and flour. Next, cook for 1 minute. Stir in the tomato paste, broth, and the rest of the ingredients. Then cover and cook for 1 hour on low heat. Uncover and cook for 15 minutes on a simmer. Adjust the seasoning with black pepper and salt. Finally, remove the thyme. Serve.

Berry's Irish Stew

Preparation time: 15 minutes
Cook time: 2 hours 11 minutes
Nutrition facts (per serving): 438 Cal (22g fat, 27g protein, 1g fiber)

This stew is always an easy way to add extra flavors and nutrients to your menu. Plus, you can make in just a few minutes.

Ingredients (8 servings)
2 tablespoons plain flour
2 ¼ lbs. neck fillet of lamb, diced
3 tablespoons oil
2 onions, sliced
2 celery sticks, sliced
3 medium carrots, peeled and sliced
2 bay leaves
1 tablespoon thyme leaves, chopped
1-pint chicken stock
1 ¾ lbs. floury potatoes, peeled and sliced
Salt and black pepper, to taste

Preparation
At 350 degrees F, preheat your oven. Toss the lamb with black pepper, flour, and salt in a bowl. Sauté the lamb in a suitable cooking pot with oil for 6 minutes until brown in batches and then transfer to a plate. Add more oil, carrots, celery, and onions to the same pot and sauté for 5 minutes. Stir in the lamb, thyme, bay leaves, and stock. Next, cook to a boil. Reduce its heat, add potatoes, and cover to cook for 2 hours. Serve warm.

Soy Irish Stew

Preparation time: 15 minutes

Cook time: 35 minutes

Nutrition facts (per serving): 679 Cal (13g fat, 25g protein, 3g fiber)

Here's a delicious and savory combination of soy chunks, carrots, and potatoes that you must add to your menu.

Ingredients (6 servings)

2 tablespoon sunflower oil

1 Spanish onion, sliced

2 leeks, sliced

2 stalks celery, diced

1 teaspoon fresh thyme leaves

1 large bay leaf

3 medium carrots cut into chunks

1 lb. new or baby potatoes, cut in half

1 vegetable broth

4 oz. dried soy chunks, soaked

2 tablespoon fresh parsley chopped

Preparations

Sauté the carrots, bay leaves, thyme, celery, leeks, and onion with oil in a suitable pan for 10 minutes. Stir in the rest of the stew ingredients, cook to a boil, reduce the heat, and cook on a simmer for 25 minutes. Serve warm.

Corned Beef and Cabbage

Preparation time: 15 minutes
Cook time: 3 hours 25 minutes
Nutrition facts (per serving): 344 Cal (6g fat, 28g protein, 5g fiber)

If you haven't tried the corned beef and cabbage recipe before, then here comes a simple and easy to cook recipe that you can recreate at home in no time with minimum efforts.

Ingredients (6 servings)

3 lbs. corned beef brisket

2 bay leaves

4 sprigs thyme

½ lb. baby potatoes, quartered

4 medium carrots, cut into quarters

1 green cabbage head, cut into wedges

Preparation

Add the brisket and enough water to cover it to a Dutch oven. Add the thyme, bay leaves and spice packet, cook to a boil, reduce its heat, and cook for 3 hours, while adding more water if needed. Stir in the carrots and the potatoes, cook to a boil, and cook for 15 minutes. Stir in the cabbage and then cook for 5 minutes. Serve warm.

Shepherd's Pie

Preparation time: 15 minutes
Cook time: 55 minutes
Nutrition facts (per serving): 336 Cal (13g fat,28g protein, 1.7g fiber)

A perfect mix of potato topping and beef filling inside is worth trying. Serve warm with your favorite side salad for the best taste.

Ingredients (6 servings)

Potatoes
1 ½ lbs. potatoes, peeled
Salt, to taste
4 tablespoon butter, melted
¼ cup milk
¼ cup sour cream
Black pepper, to taste

Beef Mixture
1 tablespoon olive oil
1 large onion, chopped
2 carrots, peeled and chopped
2 garlic cloves, minced
1 teaspoon fresh thyme
1 ½ lb. ground beef
1 cup frozen peas
1 cup frozen corn
2 tablespoon all-purpose flour
⅔ cup chicken broth
1 tablespoon parsley, chopped

Preparation

At 400 degrees F, preheat your oven. Add the potatoes, water, and a pinch of salt to a cooking pot and boil them for 18 minutes until soft. Drain and mash the potatoes in a bowl. Stir in the milk, sour cream, butter, black pepper, and salt and then mix well. Sauté the onions, carrots, garlic and thyme with oil in a large cooking pot for 5 minutes. Stir in the ground beef and then sauté for 5 minutes. Add corn and peas and then cook for 1 minute. Stir in the chicken broth and cook for 5 minutes. Spread this beef mixture in a casserole dish and add the potato mash on top in an even layer. Bake the prepared pie for 20 minutes in the oven and garnish with parsley. Serve warm.

Vegan Shepherd's Pie

Preparation time: 15 minutes
Cook time: 71 minutes
Nutrition facts (per serving): 316 Cal (7g fat, 24g protein, 12g fiber)

The Irish vegan shepherd's pie is famous for its crispy texture, unique taste, and delectable aroma, and now you can bring those exotic flavors home by using this recipe.

Ingredients (8 servings)
Potatoes
1 ½ lb. potatoes, peeled
Salt, to taste
4 tablespoon melted butter
¼ cup milk
¼ cup sour cream
Black pepper, to taste

Filling
1 tablespoon olive oil
1 large onion, chopped
2 carrots, peeled and chopped
2 garlic cloves, minced
1 teaspoon fresh thyme
1 ½ lb. butternut squash, peeled and diced
1 cup mushrooms, sliced
2 tablespoon all-purpose flour
⅔ cup chicken broth
1 tablespoon parsley, chopped

Preparation

At 400 degrees F, preheat your oven. Add the potatoes, water, and a pinch of salt to a cooking pot and boil them for 18 minutes until soft. Drain and mash the potatoes in a bowl. Stir in the milk, sour cream, butter, black pepper and salt and then mix well. Sauté the onions, carrots, garlic, and thyme with oil in a large cooking pot for 5 minutes. Stir in the butternut squash and then sauté for 7 minutes. Add the corn and peas and then cook for 1 minute. Stir in the chicken broth and cook for 5 minutes. Spread this squash mixture in a casserole dish and add the potato mash on top in an even layer. Bake the pie for 35 minutes in the oven and garnish with parsley. Serve warm.

Corned Beef and Cabbage Sliders

Preparation time: 15 minutes

Cook time: 24 minutes

Nutrition facts (per serving): 342 Cal (17g fat, 38g protein, 0g fiber)

Are you in a mood to have corned beef on the menu? Well, you can serve these delicious, corned beef and cabbage sliders.

Ingredients (8 servings)

1 tablespoon olive oil

1 head cabbage, cut into small wedges

1 bottle Guinness beer

8 ciabatta rolls

1 jar Dijon mustard

1 lb. corned beef

Preparation

At 350 degrees F, preheat your oven. Sauté the cabbage wedges with oil in a suitable skillet for 1 minute per side. Allow the cabbages to cool. Pour the Guinness over the cabbages, place them on a baking sheet, and then roast for 22 minutes. Cut the ciabatta rolls in half; add the cabbage, corned beef, and Dijon mustard to the rolls. Serve.

Unstuffed Cabbage Casserole

Preparation time: 10 minutes
Cook time: 67 minutes
Nutrition facts (per serving): 425 Cal (28g fat, 33g protein, 2g fiber)

Have you tried the Irish cabbage casserole before? Well, now you can enjoy this unique and flavorsome combination by cooking this recipe at home.

Ingredients (8 servings)

Cooking spray
1 large head cabbage, chopped
2 tablespoon olive oil
1 large onion, chopped
3 garlic cloves, minced
1 lb. ground beef
2 tablespoon tomato paste
1 (14.5-oz.) can chopped tomatoes
1 cup rice
3 cup chicken broth

Preparation

At 350 degrees F, preheat your oven. Layer a 9x13 inches baking dish with cooking spray. Sauté the onion with oil in a Dutch oven for 5 minutes. Add the garlic and then sauté for 1 minute. Stir in the ground beef and sauté for 6 minutes. Add the tomato paste, rice, 2 cups broth, black pepper, salt, and oregano and then cook for 10 minutes. Add the cabbage and cook for 5 minutes. Add the remaining 1 cup broth and then spread this rice mixture in the baking dish. Finally, cover with a foil sheet and bake for 40 minutes. Garnish with parsley and serve warm.

Reuben Nachos

Preparation time: 15 minutes
Cook time: 15 minutes
Nutrition facts (per serving): 443 Cal (16g fat, 23g protein, 0.6g fiber)

This recipe is great to complete your Irish menu.

Ingredients (6 servings)
1 bag bagel chips
½ lb. deli corned beef, chopped
½ cup sauerkraut
1 ½ cup Swiss cheese, shredded
1 tablespoon horseradish
Russian dressing, for serving
2 tablespoon chives, chopped

Preparation
At 350 degrees F, preheat your oven. Spread half of the bagel chips on a baking sheet and top them with half of the sauerkraut, horseradish, and cheese. Then add the remaining chips on top. Add the remaining cheese, horseradish, and sauerkraut on top and bake for 15 minutes. Garnish with chives and Russian dressing. Serve warm.

Corned Beef Brisket

Preparation time: 15 minutes
Cook time: 3 hours
Nutrition facts (per serving): 338 Cal (10g fat, 33g protein, 3g fiber)

Now you can quickly make a flavorsome Irish corned beef at home and serve it for a fancy meal for yourself and your guest.

Ingredients (6 servings)

3 lbs. corned beef brisket
½ teaspoon whole allspice berries
½ teaspoon coriander seeds
½ teaspoon whole cloves
¼ cup brown sugar
2 teaspoon black pepper

Preparation

At 325 degrees f, preheat your oven. Rinse the beef and it place on a roasting rack, set in a roasting pan. Grind cloves with coriander and allspice in a mortar using a pestle. Mix these spices with brown sugar and black pepper. Drizzle this spice mixture over the brisket and rub it well. Add 6 cups of water to the pan, cover the beef brisket with a foil sheet, and then roast it for 2 hours. Uncover and roast for 1 hour. Slice and serve warm.

Barbecue Pulled Pork Shepherd's Pie

Preparation time: 10 minutes
Cook time: 16 minutes
Nutrition facts (per serving): 378 Cal (11g fat, 25g protein, 3g fiber)

If you haven't tried the pulled pork pie before, then here comes a simple and easy to cook recipe that you can recreate at home in no time with minimum efforts.

Ingredients (8 servings)
Mashed Potatoes
2 lb. red potatoes
½ packet ranch seasoning mix
⅔ cup sour cream

Filling
1 lb. pulled pork
1 bottle barbecue sauce
1 can corn, juices drained
1 cup Cheddar cheese, shredded
1 bunch scallions, diced

Preparation
At 400 degrees F, preheat your oven. Peel and dice all the red potatoes and then add them to a cooking pot. Pour in water, add a pinch of salt, and then boil until the potatoes are soft. Drain and mash the potatoes in a bowl. Stir in the sour cream and the ranch seasoning and then mix well. Mix the pulled pork with corn, scallions, and barbecue sauce in a casserole dish. Spread the mashed

THE ULTIMATE IRISH COOKBOOK |109

potatoes on top and then drizzle cheese on top. Bake this pie for 16 minutes until the cheese is melted. Serve warm.

Reuben Wraps

Preparation time: 10 minutes

Cook time: 5 minutes

Nutrition facts (per serving): 391 Cal (7g fat, 27g protein, 2g fiber)

Try to make these delicious wraps with a unique combination of cabbage and corned beef at home to enjoy the best of the Irish flavors!

Ingredients (6 servings)

6 leaves cabbage

12 slices Swiss cheese

¼ lb. corned beef, sliced

1 cup sauerkraut

¼ cup Russian dressing, for dipping

Preparation

Boil about 4 cups water in a cooking pot and add the cabbage leaves to this water for 30 seconds. Next, transfer to a plate lined with a paper towel. Add 2 cheese slices on top of each cabbage leaf and evenly divide beef and sauerkraut on top of all the leaves and roll them like a burrito. Serve with Russian dressing.

Reuben Bowls

Preparation time: 10 minutes
Cook time: 13 minutes
Nutrition facts (per serving): 396 Cal (13g fat, 22g protein, 4g fiber)

This loaded bowl brings all the delicious Irish delights in one place, including cabbage, carrots, and corned beef.

Ingredients (4 servings)
Dressing
¼ cup mayonnaise
2 tablespoon sweet pickle relish
4 teaspoon ketchup
1 ½ teaspoon prepared horseradish
1 teaspoon fresh lemon juice
½ teaspoon Worcestershire sauce
Salt, to taste
Black pepper, to taste

Bowl
2 teaspoon caraway seeds
1 tablespoon olive oil
½ yellow onion, chopped
¼ green cabbage, sliced
1 cup shredded carrot
¾ lb. corned beef, sliced
1 ½ cup sauerkraut, drained
1 cup shredded Swiss cheese
¼ cup cornichon, sliced
1 green onion, sliced

Preparation

Mix the lemon juice, Worcestershire sauce, black pepper, salt, horseradish, ketchup, pickle relish, and mayonnaise in a small bowl. Toast the caraway seeds in a large skillet for 30 seconds, then transfer to a plate. Sauté the onion with oil in the same skillet for 3 minutes. Stir in the black pepper, salt, carrot and cabbage and then sauté for 5 minutes. Add sauerkraut and corned beef and then sauté for 1 minute. Top the mixture with Swiss cheese, cover, and cook for 3 minutes. Garnish with the caraway seeds and cornichon. Finally, garnish with dressing and green onion. Serve warm.

Cheesy Cabbage Gratin

Preparation time: 10 minutes
Cook time: 80 minutes
Nutrition facts (per serving): 392 Cal (13g fat, 19g protein, 0.5g fiber)

This cheese cabbage gratin makes a flavorsome serving with bread for your dinner or as a good, delicious lunch.

Ingredients (4 servings)
1 green cabbage, cut into 8 wedges
2 tablespoon olive oil
Salt, to taste
Black pepper, to taste
2 cup heavy cream
3 garlic cloves, grated
¼ teaspoon ground nutmeg
½ cup Parmesan cheese, grated
4 sprigs thyme
1 cup gouda, shredded

Preparation
At 350 degrees F, preheat your oven. Toss the cabbage wedges with black pepper, salt, and oil on a baking sheet. Roast them for 45 minutes and flip once cooked halfway through. Mix the Parmesan, nutmeg, garlic, and cream in a medium bowl. Spread the cabbage in a medium baking dish and then pour the cream sauce over the cabbage. Add the thyme sprigs and the Gouda on top. Roast the cabbage for 30 minutes. Serve warm.

Irish Stew Pie

Preparation time: 10 minutes
Cook time: 85 minutes
Nutrition facts (per serving): 731 Cal (40g fat, 24g protein, 5g fiber)

This pie is one delicious way to complete your Irish menu. In turn, here's a recipe that you can try for a delicious meal.

Ingredients (8 servings)

½ cup 1 tablespoon all-purpose flour

¾ teaspoon salt

¾ teaspoon black pepper

1 lb. boneless lamb shoulder, cubed

2 tablespoon canola oil

2 medium carrots, chopped

1 onion, halved and sliced

1 ¼ cups beef stock

2 Yukon Gold potatoes, peeled and cubed

1 fresh thyme sprig

1 bay leaf

1 teaspoon Worcestershire sauce

1 teaspoon tomato paste

3 tablespoon fresh mint, chopped

1 large egg yolk

2 tablespoon heavy whipping cream

1 package (17.3 oz.) frozen puff pastry, thawed

Preparation

At 350 degrees F, preheat your oven. Spread 1 puff pastry sheet in a 9-inch pie plate. Mix the lamb with ½ cup flour, ⅔ teaspoon black pepper and ⅔ teaspoon salt in a bowl. Next, then shake off the excess. Sauté the beef with oil in a suitable pan until brown and then transfer to a plate. Add the onion and the carrots to the same pan and sauté for 8 minutes. Stir in 1 tablespoon flour and mix well. Pour in the stock and cook to a boil while mixing well. Add lamb, ¼ teaspoon black pepper, ¼ teaspoon black pepper, tomato paste, Worcestershire sauce, bay leaf, thyme, and potatoes. Then cook to a boil. Reduce its heat and cook for 30 minutes on a simmer until it thickens. Discard the thyme and the bay leaf. Add the mint, stir well, and spread the mixture onto the pie plate. Beat the egg yolk with cream in a bowl and brush over the pie crusts edges. Spread the other puff pastry sheet on top and pinch to seal. Cut 2-3 slits on top of the puff pastry and brush the egg mixture on top. Bake the pie for 40 minutes in the oven. Serve warm.

Saucy Beef Cabbage Supper

Preparation time: 10 minutes
Cook time: 23 minutes
Nutrition facts (per serving): 260 Cal (13g fat, 17g protein, 4g fiber)

Let's make a cabbage supper with these simple ingredients. Mix them together and then cook to achieve great flavors.

Ingredients (4 servings)

1-lb. lean ground beef

1 medium onion, chopped

2 large garlic cloves, minced

1 small head cabbage, chopped

5 medium carrots, peeled and diced

3 tablespoon olive oil

1 teaspoon salt

1 teaspoon black pepper

½ teaspoon caraway seeds

¼ teaspoon ground allspice

⅛ teaspoon ground cloves

½ cup ketchup

2 teaspoon cider vinegar

Preparation

Sauté the beef with the garlic and the onion with oil in a stockpot for 7 minutes. Stir in the seasonings, carrots, and cabbage and then sauté for 11 minutes. Stir in vinegar and ketchup and then cook for 5 minutes. Serve warm.

Rutabaga Pie

Preparation time: 10 minutes
Cook time: 60 minutes
Nutrition facts (per serving): 394 Cal (19 g fat, 13g protein, 1g fiber)

Count on Rutabaga pie to make your dinner extra special and surprise your loved one with the ultimate flavors.

Ingredients (8 servings)

3 cups peeled rutabagas, diced
2 cups peeled potatoes, diced
1 lb. ground beef
½ cup onion, chopped
½ cup celery, sliced
¼ cup steak sauce
1 teaspoon salt
¼ teaspoon black pepper
Pastry for double-crust pie (9 inches)

Preparation

Boil the potatoes and the rutabagas in a pot filled with salted water and cook until soft. Drain the veggies and keep them aside. Sauté the celery, onion, and beef with oil in cooking until beef turns brown. Stir in the potatoes, rutabagas, black pepper, and salt. Layer a 9-inch pie pan with a puff pastry sheet. Spread the rutabaga mixture in the pastry and spread the other sheet on top. Pinch the edges and cut slits on top. Bake the pie for 10 minutes at 425 degrees F. Reduce its heat to 350 degrees, then bake for 40 minutes. Serve warm.

Lemon-Parsley Baked Cod

Preparation time: 10 minutes

Cook time: 15 minutes

Nutrition facts (per serving): 232 Cal (10g fat, 28g protein, 6g fiber)

This baked cod will melt your heart away with its epic flavors. This fish is filled with savory lemon flavors.

Ingredients (4 servings)

3 tablespoon lemon juice

3 tablespoon butter, melted

¼ cup all-purpose flour

½ teaspoon salt

¼ teaspoon paprika

¼ teaspoon lemon-pepper seasoning

4 cod fillets (6 oz.)

2 tablespoon fresh parsley, minced

2 teaspoon lemon zest, grated

Preparation

At 400 degrees F, preheat your oven. Mix the butter with lemon juice in a shallow bowl. Mix the seasonings with flour in another bowl. First, dip the cod fillets in the lemon mixture and then coat with the flour mixture and shake off the excess. Place the coated cod in a 13x9 inch baking dish, drizzle lemon mixture on top, and then bake for 15 minutes in the oven. Garnish with lemon zest and parsley. Serve warm.

Braised Short Ribs

Preparation time: 10 minutes
Cook time: 7 hours 2 minutes
Nutrition facts (per serving): 281 Cal (14g fat, 22g protein, 1g fiber)

If you haven't tried the Irish braised short ribs before, then here comes a simple and easy to cook recipe that you can recreate at home in no time with minimum efforts.

Ingredients (8 servings)
½ cup all-purpose flour
1 ½ teaspoon salt
1 ½ teaspoon paprika
½ teaspoon ground mustard
4 lbs. bone-in beef short ribs
2 tablespoon canola oil
2 medium onions, sliced
1 cup beer
1 garlic clove, minced

Gravy
2 teaspoon all-purpose flour
1 tablespoon cold water

Preparation
Mix the flour with the mustard, paprika, and salt in a shallow dish. Coat the ribs with this flour mixture and sear them in a skillet with oil until brown. Transfer the ribs to a plate. Add the ribs, onions, garlic, and beer to a slow cooker, cover,

and cook for 7 hours on low heat. Transfer the cooked ribs and onions to a plate. Boil the remaining liquid and mix flour with water. Pour into the cooker and cook for 2 minutes until it thickens. Pour this sauce over the ribs. Serve warm.

Triple Mash with Horseradish Breadcrumbs

Preparation time: 15 minutes
Cook time: 35 minutes
Nutrition facts (per serving): 119 Cal (9g fat, 4g protein, 0.5g fiber)

The famous triple mash recipe is here to make your Irish cuisine extra special. Serve it with flatbreads for the best taste.

Ingredients (6 servings)

1 ¾ lbs. Yukon Gold potatoes, peeled and cubed

4 medium parsnips, peeled and cubed

2-½ cups peeled rutabaga, cubed

2 teaspoon salt

½ cup butter

1 cup soft breadcrumbs

2 tablespoon horseradish

1 cup whole milk

¼ teaspoon black pepper

Preparation

Add the rutabagas, parsnips, salt, and potatoes to a Dutch oven and enough water to cover. Cook to a boil, reduce its heat, and cook for 20 minutes. Sauté the breadcrumbs with ¼ cup butter in a skillet for 5 minutes. Add the horseradish and remove from the heat. Drain the cooked veggies and return them to the Dutch oven. Mash the veggies and add the remaining butter, black pepper, and milk, then mix well. Spread the vegetable mixture on a plate and top with the breadcrumbs on top. Serve.

Seafood Chowder

Preparation time: 10 minutes
Cook time: 23 minutes
Nutrition facts (per serving): 390 Cal (23g fat, 28g protein,6 g fiber)

This Irish seafood chowder recipe has unique flavors due to its rich blend of shrimp with creamy base. Serve warm with rice or bread.

Ingredients (6 servings)
3 tablespoon ¼ cup butter
1-lb. fresh mushrooms, sliced
⅓ cup all-purpose flour
1 teaspoon salt
⅛ teaspoon black pepper
4 cups half-and-half cream
1 ½ cups milk
1 lb. haddock fillets, cut into 1-inch pieces
1 lb. medium shrimp, peeled and deveined
2 cups frozen peas
¾ cup Cheddar cheese, shredded
1 cup lump crabmeat, drained
1 jar (4 oz.) diced pimientos, drained
1 teaspoon paprika

Preparation
Sauté the mushrooms with 3 tablespoon butter in a stockpot for 10 minutes, over medium-high heat. Transfer these mushrooms to a plate. Add the remaining butter, black pepper, salt, and flour then mix well. Pour in the milk

and cream and then cook to a boil. Reduce its heat and cook on a simmer for 3 minutes. Add the shrimp, peas, sautéed mushrooms, and haddock. Next, cook for 7 minutes. Add the pimientos, crab, and cheese, and then cook for 3 minutes. Garnish with paprika, then serve warm.

Stout and Shiitake Pot Roast

Preparation time: 10 minutes

Cook time: 2 hours

Nutrition facts (per serving): 441 Cal (21g fat, 33g protein, 3g fiber)

Best to serve at dinner, this pot roast offers as an energizing meal. It's an Irish version of delicious pot roast.

Ingredients (6 servings)

3 tablespoon olive oil

1 boneless beef chuck roast

2 medium onions, sliced

1 garlic clove, minced

1 bottle (12 oz.) stout

½ oz. dried shiitake mushrooms

1 tablespoon brown sugar

1 teaspoon Worcestershire sauce

½ teaspoon dried savory

1 lb. red potatoes, diced

2 medium carrots, sliced

½ cup water

½ teaspoon salt

¼ teaspoon black pepper

Preparation

Sear the roast with 1 tablespoon oil in a Dutch oven until brown from all the sides. Next, transfer to a plate. Add more oil, garlic, and onions and then sauté until soft. Stir in the beef and deglaze. Add savory, Worcestershire sauce, brown sugar, and mushrooms. Then return the roast. Cook the mixture to a boil, reduce its heat, cover, and cook for 1 ½ hour on a simmer. Add the rest of the ingredients and cook for 25 minutes with occasional stirring and then serve warm.

Shepherd's Pie with Mashed Cauliflower

Preparation time: 15 minutes

Cook time: 40 minutes

Nutrition facts (per serving): 456 Cal (15g fat, 26g protein, 0.7g fiber)

If you haven't tried this shepherd's pie, then here comes a simple and easy to cook recipe that you can recreate at home in no time with minimum efforts.

Ingredients (6 servings)

2 tablespoon olive oil

1 medium yellow onion, chopped

1 small red pepper, chopped

1 tablespoon jalapeno, minced

2 garlic cloves, minced

1 lb. ground turkey

Salt, to taste

Black pepper, to taste

1 tablespoon chilli powder

1 (14.5 oz.) can fire-roasted tomatoes, diced

½ cup corn kernels

1 (20 oz.) bag mashed cauliflower, cheddar, and bacon, cooked

2 green onions, sliced

Preparation

At 425 degrees F, preheat your oven. Sauté the red pepper and onion with oil in a suitable pot for 5 minutes. Stir in the garlic and jalapeno and then sauté for 2 minutes. Stir in the turkey and sauté for 8 minutes. Add the chili powder, tomatoes, corn, and salt. Next, cook for 5 minutes on a simmer. Mix the cauliflower mixture with white parts of green onion in a bowl. Spread the turkey mixture in a casserole dish and top t with a cauliflower mixture. Bake for 20 minutes and garnish with green onion. Serve warm.

Corned Beef Grilled Cheese

Preparation time: 15 minutes

Cook time: 35 minutes

Nutrition facts (per serving): 419 Cal (14g fat, 19g protein, 7g fiber)

Irish corned beef grilled cheese is one option to go for in dinner. Sure, it takes some time to get it ready, but it's a great taste worth all the time and effort.

Ingredients (4 servings)

1 ½ tablespoon butter

2 medium yellow onion, sliced

1 ½ tablespoon sugar

⅛ teaspoon caraway seeds

Salt and black pepper, to taste

1 cup dark beer

8 oz. deli-sliced corn beef, cut into strips

1 tablespoon Worcestershire sauce

1 tablespoon whole-grain mustard

2 cups Jarlsberg cheese, shredded

8 marble rye bread slices

Butter for grilling sandwiches

Preparation

Sauté the onion with 1 ½ tablespoon butter, ¼ teaspoon black pepper, and ½ teaspoon salt in a cooking pan for 15 minutes until soft. Stir in the beer and sauté for 10 minutes. Remove it from the heat and add the mustard, Worcestershire sauce, and corned beef slices. Divide the corned beef and onion mixture and cheese on top of 4 bread slices. Place the other bread slices on top and brush the butter over the sandwiches. Grill the sandwiches for 5 minutes per side in a grill pan. Serve warm.

Beef Stew with Cheddar Dumplings

Preparation time: 5 minutes
Cook time: 3 hours
Nutrition facts (per serving): 376 Cal (14g fat, 22g protein, 18g fiber)

This Irish beef stew with dumpling recipe will make your day with a delightful taste. Serve warm with your favorite bread.

Ingredients (6 servings)
Stew
¼ lb. bacon
2 lbs. boneless beef chuck, diced
Salt and black pepper, to taste
4 sticks celery, chopped
3 large carrots, chopped
1 large onion, chopped
4 garlic cloves, minced
2 large potatoes or parsnips, diced
1 turnip, diced
3 oz. tomato paste
1 (12 oz.) bottle Guinness
4 cups chicken broth
2 tablespoon Worcestershire sauce
1 bay leaf
3 sprigs thyme
1 tablespoon cornstarch, or as needed
½ lb. cremini mushrooms, sliced
Chopped parsley

Cheddar Herb Dumplings

1 ½ cups self-rising flour

½ teaspoon garlic powder

⅓ cup shortening

¾ cup Irish sharp cheddar, shredded

⅔ cup milk

2 tablespoon mixed fresh herbs, chopped

Preparation

Sauté the bacon in a heavy-based pan until crispy and then transfer to a plate. Add the beef, black pepper, and salt to the bacon fat and sauté until brown. Transfer the beef to the bacon. Sauté the carrots, celery, and onion in the same pan until soft. Stir in the garlic and then sauté for 30 seconds. Add the tomato paste. Add the Worcestershire sauce and Guinness; then cook on a simmer. Return the cooked beef to the pan and add the broth, the thyme, and the bay leaf. Cover and cook on a simmer for 1 ½ hour. Add the potatoes and the turnip and then cook 30 minutes. Discard the thyme and the bay leaf. Mix 1 tablespoon cold water and cornstarch in a bowl. Pour this slurry into the stew and cook until it thickens. Stir in the mushrooms and cook for 10 minutes. Add the bacon to the stew.

At 350 degrees F, preheat your oven. Mix the garlic powder with self-rising flour in a medium bowl. Cut in the shortening and mix until crumbly. Add the cheddar cheese and milk; then mix evenly. Make small dough balls from this mixture. Finally, add the dumplings to the stew and bake this stew for 40 minutes. Garnish with parsley and serve warm.

Irish Cabbage and Bacon

Preparation time: 15 minutes

Cook time: 30 minutes

Nutrition facts (per serving): 349 Cal (7g fat, 29g protein, 3g fiber)

If you want some new flavors in your meals, then this cabbage and bacon recipe is best to bring variety to the menu.

Ingredients (4 servings)

24 ounces thick-cut bacon, chopped

1 large green cabbage

1 large onion

2 ½ cups chicken broth

1 tablespoon mustard seeds

Salt and pepper

Preparation

Place a suitable cooking pan over medium heat. Sauté the bacon until crispy. Stir in the onion and sauté for 4 minutes. Add the cabbage, broth, mustard seeds, black pepper, and salt. Lastly, cook for 20 minutes. Serve warm.

Irish Cheddar Macaroni Cheese

Preparation time: 5 minutes
Cook time: 25 minutes
Nutrition facts (per serving): 543 Cal (26g fat, 22g protein, 0.3g fiber)

Here's a special Irish mac and cheese, which is great to serve at festive dinners and holiday celebrations. The macaroni is mixed with cream cheese and then cooked into a delicious meal.

Ingredients (6 servings)

1-lb. elbow macaroni

2 tablespoon butter

2 tablespoon flour

⅔ cup Guinness

1 ½ cups (2%) milk

½ cup half and half

½ teaspoon salt

¼ teaspoon ground black pepper

1 tablespoon Dijon mustard

2 oz. cream cheese, cut into pieces

3 ½ cups cheddar, grated

Topping

1 tablespoon butter

2 teaspoon garlic, minced

½ cup panko breadcrumbs

Salt and black pepper, to taste

2 teaspoon fresh parsley, minced

Preparation

For the topping, sauté the garlic with breadcrumbs and butter a suitable skillet until golden. Stir in the black pepper, salt, and parsley and then keep it aside. Boil the elbow macaroni in salted salt until soft, drain, and reserve the ½ cup cooking liquid. Sauté the melted butter with flour in a large saucepan over medium heat for 1 minute. Stir in the milk, half and half, black pepper, salt, mustard, and Guinness. Next, mix evenly and cook until it thickens. Stir in 2 ½ cups cheddar and cream cheese and then mix until smooth. Stir in the cooked pasta and the remaining 1 cup cheddar. Finally, cook until the cheese is melted. Garnish with toasted breadcrumbs and serve warm.

Dublin Coddle

Preparation time: 15 minutes
Cook time: 65 minutes
Nutrition facts (per serving): 411 Cal (9g fat, 11g protein, 7g fiber)

When you can't think of anything to serve in the lunch or dinner, then these Irish Dublin coddles will help you big time to enjoy the authentic Irish flavors.

Ingredients (6 servings)

3 cups beef broth

1 lb. smoked sausages, cut into rounds

½ lb. smoked bacon, chopped

2 lbs. russet potatoes, peeled and sliced

2 yellow onions, sliced

3 large carrots, sliced

Salt and black pepper, to taste

2 tablespoon fresh parsley, chopped

Preparation

At 425 degrees F, preheat your oven. Mix the sliced sausages, bacon, and beef broth in a large saucepan and then cook to a boil. Reduce its heat and cook for 10 minutes on a simmer. Transfer this mixture to a bowl. Set this broth aside. Grease a casserole dish with cooking spray. Spread ⅓ potatoes in the casserole dish and top them with ⅓ onions and carrots on top. Drizzle black pepper and salt on top. Spread the bacon and sausage on top. Repeat the layers and pour the prepared sauce on top. Cover and bake for 40 minutes in the oven. Uncover and cook for 15 minutes. Garnish with parsley and serve warm.

Maple Mustard Corned Beef

Preparation time: 10 minutes

Cook time: 7 hours 10 minutes

Nutrition facts (per serving): 326 Cal (17g fat, 14g protein, 1.2g fiber)

Here's another classic recipe for your dinner, lunch, or snack collection. Serve it with a delicious entree and enjoy the best of it.

Ingredients (6 servings)

3 lbs. flat cut corned beef roast (minus the spice packet)

2 teaspoon cooking oil

½ cup maple syrup

¼ cup yellow mustard

¼ teaspoon black pepper

1 garlic clove minced

Preparation

Pat dry the corned beef with a paper towel. Sauté this meat with oil in a suitable until brown. Transfer this mixture to a slow cooker. Mix the garlic cloves, black pepper, mustard, and maple syrup in a small bowl and pour over the corned beef. Finally, cover and then cook for 7 hours on low heat. Serve warm.

Bacon Corned Beef Burgers

Preparation time: 10 minutes
Cook time: 33 minutes
Nutrition facts (per serving): 567 Cal (26g fat, 29g protein, 1.2g fiber)

Try this super tasty beef burger to dazzle all. The juicy corned beef burger can be served with fried eggs in a bun.

Ingredients (4 servings)
1 tablespoon oil
1 large onion, sliced
1 cup Guinness
1 teaspoon Worcestershire sauce
2 teaspoon grainy mustard
8 strips bacon
1 ½ lbs. corned beef, ground
4 slices white cheddar cheese
4 buns

Preparation
Sauté the onions with oil in a cooking pan for 7 minutes. Stir in ¼ cup Guinness, cover, and cook for 15 minutes on a simmer. Stir in the mustard and Worcestershire sauce. Add the cooked bacon and beef then mix well. Allow the mixture to cool and then make 4 patties from this mixture. Sear the patties in a skillet, greased with cooking oil, for 5 minutes per side. Place one patty between each bun, cut in half, and add a cheese slice. Serve.

Desserts

Irish Apple Cake with Warm Custard Sauce

Preparation time: 10 minutes
Cook time: 54 minutes
Nutrition facts (per serving): 379 Cal (11g fat, 4g protein, 3g fiber)

If you haven't tried the Irish apple cake before, then here comes a simple and easy to cook recipe that you can recreate at home in no time with minimum efforts.

Ingredients (6 servings)
Cake
3 cups cake flour
¾ cup granulated sugar
2 teaspoon baking powder
½ teaspoon salt
¼ teaspoon nutmeg
⅛ teaspoon cloves
½ cup butter, melted and cooled
¼ cup vegetable oil
2 eggs
¾ cup whole milk
1 teaspoon vanilla
4 Granny Smith apples, peeled and diced
2 tablespoon granulated sugar

Custard Sauce
1 ½ cup whole milk
½ cup granulated sugar
6 large egg yolks
2 teaspoon vanilla extract

Preparation

At 375 degrees F, preheat your oven. Layer a 9-inch springform pan with cooking spray. Mix the flour with nutmeg, cloves, salt, baking powder, sugar, and cake flour in a large bowl. Beat the eggs with vanilla, milk, oil and butter in another bowl. Stir in the flour mixture and then mix until smooth. Stir in the apples, spread this mixture in the pan, and bake for 50 minutes in the oven. Boil the milk in a cooking pot until it bubbles. Beat the egg yolks with sugar in a bowl for 3 minutes until pale. Pour the egg yolk into the hot milk and cook until the mixture thickens for 4 minutes. Add vanilla and pour this sauce over the cake and allow the cake to cool. Refrigerate the cake for 1 hour. Slice and serve.

Irish Porter Cake

Preparation time: 15 minutes

Cook time: 1 hour 6 minutes

Nutrition facts (per serving): 347 Cal (5g fat, 7g protein, 5g fiber)

A dessert that has no parallel, the Irish porter cake is made with flour, cinnamon, and egg batter, which give it a super soft and moist texture.

Ingredients (6 servings)

1 cup unsalted butter

1 cup dark brown sugar

Zest of 1 orange

Zest of 1 lemon

1 bottle (12 fl oz) porter ale

3 cups mixed dried fruit

3 ½ cups all-purpose flour

½ teaspoon baking soda

1 teaspoon baking powder

¼ teaspoon salt

½ teaspoon cinnamon

¼ teaspoon ground allspice

¼ teaspoon ground ginger

½ teaspoon nutmeg

¼ teaspoon ground cloves

¼ teaspoon ground coriander

3 eggs, beaten

Preparation

Boil the butter with lemon zest, beer, orange zest, and brown sugar in a saucepan and then cook for 3 minutes. Reduce its heat and stir in the dried fruit. Next, cook for 3 minutes. Remove this mixture from the heat. At 350 degrees F, preheat your oven. Layer a 9-inch springform pan with wax paper ad grease it. Mix the flour with spices, salt, baking powder, and baking soda in a large bowl. Stir in the fruit liquid and mix evenly. Beat the eggs and mix well. Spread this batter in the prepared pan and bake for 1 hour. Pour the stout over the cake and allow the cake to cool for 20 minutes. Serve.

Old Fashioned Potato Candy

Preparation time: 15 minutes
Cook time: 10 minutes
Nutrition facts (per serving): 221 Cal (3 g fat, 4 g protein, 2.8g fiber)

Yes, you can make something as delicious as these Irish potato candies by using only basic dessert ingredients and some simple techniques.

Ingredients (8 servings)
1 small potato, peeled and cut into pieces
8 cups powdered sugar
⅔ cup peanut butter
½ teaspoon vanilla

Preparation
Boil the potato with water in a cooking pot until soft and then drain. Mash the boiled potatoes in a bowl until lump-free. Stir in 4 cups powder sugar and mix until the sugar is dissolved. Spread the potato mixture in the baking pan, lined with parchment paper, into ¼ inch thick rectangle. Add the peanut butter on top, cover, and then refrigerate for 30 minutes. Cut in squares and serve.

Irish Yellowman Candy

Preparation time: 15 minutes
Cook time: 5 minutes
Nutrition facts (per serving): 357 Cal (12g fat, 5.5g protein, 1.4g fiber)

Try this Irish yellow man candy on the menu. The sweet combination of golden syrup with brown sugar is bliss for all sweet tooth fans like I am!

Ingredients (6 servings)

16 oz. golden syrup

14 oz. light brown sugar

⅔ oz. butter

2 tablespoon white vinegar

1 tablespoon baking soda

Preparation

Layer an 8x8 inch baking pan with parchment paper. Cook the brown sugar with the melted butter in a pan until golden brown and the sugar is dissolved with occasional stirring. Remove the sugar mixture from the heat and then add white vinegar and baking soda. Mix well and pour this mixture into a greased baking pan. Allow the mixture to cool and then break it into pieces. Serve.

Irish Shortbread Cookies

Preparation time: 10 minutes
Cook time: 15 minutes
Nutrition facts (per serving): 225 Cal (17g fat, 5g protein, 0.8g fiber)

These Irish shortbread cookies will leave you spellbound due to their mildly sweet taste and the lovely combination of sugar topping.

Ingredients (12 servings)

8 oz. soft Irish butter

1 teaspoon vanilla extract

½ cup granulated sugar

1 ¾ cups all-purpose flour

¼ cup corn starch

Sugar for sprinkling

Preparation

Layer two sheet pans with wax paper. Mix the vanilla and the butter in a bowl. Stir in the sugar and mix until dissolved. Stir in the cornstarch and the flour and then mix evenly. Knead this mixture for 30 seconds until smooth and then divide this dough in half. Roll each portion into ¼ inch thick round. Cut the prepared dough portions according to the sheet pan size and place one each pan. At 350 degrees F, preheat your oven. Bake the prepared dough for 8 minutes. Drizzle the sugar on top and bake for 7 minutes until golden brown. Allow the cookies to cool and serve.

Shortbread Toffee Bars

Preparation time: 15 minutes

Cook time: 35 minutes

Nutrition facts (per serving): 257 Cal (4g fat, 11g protein, 4g fiber)

The famous shortbread toffee bars are essential on the Irish dessert menu. Try cooking them at home with these healthy ingredients and enjoy.

Ingredients (12 servings)

Shortbread

1 cup salted butter

½ cup granulated sugar

2 cups all-purpose flour

Toffee

1 cup salted butter

1 cup granulated sugar

1 (14-oz.) can sweeten condensed milk

3 tablespoon maple syrup

1 (10-oz.) bag bittersweet chocolate chips

Sea salt

Preparation

At 350 degrees F, preheat your oven. Mix the sugar with the butter in a stand mixer over medium speed for 5 minutes. Stir in the flour and then mix on low speed until crumbly. Spread this dough in an 8x11 inches baking pan and bake for 20 minutes. Next, allow the crust to cool. Mix the butter with maple syrup, condensed milk, and sugar in a saucepan and cook to a boil. Cook this mixture for 7 minutes with occasional stirring until golden brown. Pour this sauce over the shortbread crust in the baking pan. Allow it to cool and set. Melt the chocolate chips in a small saucepan and pour over the caramel layer. Drizzle sea salt on top and allow the layers to set. Cut the layers into 12 pieces and serve.

Irish Oat Cookies

Preparation time: 10 minutes

Cook time: 10 minutes

Nutrition facts (per serving): 208 Cal (10g fat, 4g protein, 0.4g fiber)

If you want something exotic on your dessert menu, then nothing can taste better than these delicious oat cookies.

Ingredients (6 servings)

1 cup unsalted butter

¾ cup brown sugar

2 egg yolks

1 ½ cups all-purpose flour

1 cup old-fashioned oats

½ teaspoon baking soda

½ teaspoon salt

Preparation

Beat the egg with water, egg yolk, and the rest of the ingredients in a mixing bowl until smooth. Divide the prepared dough into 16 pieces. Spread each piece in a rectangle and pinch the two opposite edges of each rectangle. Dust these cookies with sugar and place them on a baking sheet. Finally, bake for 10 minutes until golden brown. Serve.

Irish Bread and Butter Pudding

Preparation time: 10 minutes
Cook time: 60 minutes
Nutrition facts (per serving): 202 Cal (7g fat, 6g protein, 1.3g fiber)

If you're a bread pudding lover, then this Irish dessert recipe is the right fit for you. Try this at home and cook in no time.

Ingredients (6 servings)

12 oz. milk

¼ teaspoon ground cinnamon

4 tablespoon sugar

6 thin slices white bread

¼ cup butter, softened

3 large eggs

¼ cup raisins

Preparation

Beat the eggs with milk, cinnamon, and sugar in a large bowl. Brush the thin bread slices with butter and cut the edges of the bread. Cut each bread into triangles. Grease the baking dish with butter and spread the bread triangles in the dish. Drizzle the raisins on top. Pour the prepared egg mixture on top and bake for 1 hour at 350 degrees F. Serve.

Potato Apple Bread

Preparation time: 10 minutes

Cook time: 45 minutes

Nutrition facts (per serving): 393 Cal (18g g fat, 9g protein, 3g fiber)

The famous Irish potato apple bread is another special dessert to savor on the Irish menu. Bake it at home with these healthy ingredients and enjoy it.

Ingredients (8 servings)

1 lb. 5 oz. potato, peeled and cubed

1½ oz. butter

4 oz. plain white flour

¼ teaspoon baking powder

Salt, a sprinkle

2 apples, peeled and sliced

1¾ oz. unrefined golden caster sugar

½ teaspoon vanilla bean paste

Lemon curd, to serve

Preparation

Boil the potatoes in salted water in a cooking pot for 15 minutes, drain, and mash the potatoes with butter in a bowl. Stir in the baking powder, salt, and flour and then mix evenly. Divide this dough in two equal portions and roll this dough into 8 inch circle on a floured surface. Mix apple slices with vanilla bean paste and sugar in a bowl. Spread this mixture at the center of one dough piece around, leaving ½ inch border. Place the other dough on top and press the edges with a fork. Dust a skillet and preheat on low heat. Sear the 15 minutes potato cake in the pan and flip then cook for 15 minutes. Cut in wedges and serve with lemon curd and cream.

Orange Whiskey Soufflé Pie

Preparation time: 15 minutes
Cook time: 45 minutes
Nutrition facts (per serving): 201 Cal (6g fat, 4g protein, 0.6g fiber)

The Irish whiskey souffle pie has no parallel; this apricot filled cake roll has a delicious blend of potatoes and orange extract.

Ingredients (8 servings)

1-½ cups granulated sugar, separated
1 teaspoon orange zest, grated
1 ¼ cups Yukon gold potatoes, mashed
8 tablespoon unsalted butter, melted
4 tablespoon almond flour
1 teaspoon pure vanilla extract
1 teaspoon pure almond extract
½ teaspoon orange extract
6 large eggs
2 oz. any Irish whiskey

Preparation

At 375 degrees F, preheat your oven. Grease a 9-inch springform with melted butter and layer with parchment paper. Mix 1 ¼ cups sugar and zest in a small bowl. Beat 5 egg yolks with 1 egg in a mixer for 2 minutes until fluffy. Stir in the zest sugar mixture and then mix evenly. Stir in the melted butter, almond flour, extracts, and mashed potato. Next, mix evenly. Transfer this mixture to a bowl. Beat the egg whites until fluffy and then add to the batter. Mix well and spread in the springform pan. Bake the batter for 45 minutes. Serve.

Plum Pudding Cake

Preparation time: 10 minutes
Cook time: 2 hours 37 minutes
Nutrition facts (per serving): 550 Cal (17g fat, 5g protein, 1g fiber)

The Irish plum pudding cake is great to serve with all the hot beverages. It's quite popular for its sweet and earthy taste.

Ingredients (8 servings)

2 cups butter, softened

¾ cup packed brown sugar

3 large eggs, room temperature

¾ cup dry breadcrumbs

½ cup all-purpose flour

1 tablespoon grated orange zest

1 teaspoon ground cinnamon

½ teaspoon baking soda

½ teaspoon ground nutmeg

¼ teaspoon salt

¼ teaspoon ground cloves

2 cans (15 oz.) plums, pitted and chopped

1-¾ cups dates, chopped

1 cup golden raisins

1 cup carrots, shredded

½ cup dried currants

Hard sauce

½ cup butter softened

3 cups confectioners' sugar

¼ cup dark rum

Preparation

Grease an 8-cup pudding mold. Beat the butter and brown sugar in a large bowl for 7 minutes. Stir in eggs and beat well. Mix the breadcrumbs with cloves, salt, nutmeg, baking soda, cinnamon, orange zest, and flour in another bowl. Stir in the creamed mixture and evenly. Fold in the currants, carrots, raisins, dates, and plums. Next, mix well. Divide the batter into the molds and cover with a foil sheet tightly. Place a stockpot with up to 3-inch hot water in it and set a rack inside. Boil this water, place the molds on the rack, cover, and cook for 2 ½ hours. Beat the hard sauce ingredients in a bowl until creamy. Remove the pudding from the mold and pour the hard sauce on top. Serve.

Sticky Toffee Pudding

Preparation time: 10 minutes
Cook time: 40 minutes
Nutrition facts (per serving): 358 Cal (14g fat, 12g protein, 2g fiber)

This Irish sticky toffee pudding is worth the try as it tastes so unique and exotic. This dessert is definitely a must on the Irish menu.

Ingredients (8 servings)
Cake
4 tablespoon salted butter, melted
½ cup dark brown sugar
1 egg
½ cup half and half
2 teaspoon vanilla extract
1 cup flour
1 ½ teaspoon baking powder
¼ teaspoon salt
½ cup dates, chopped

Sauce
1 cup dark brown sugar
3 tablespoon cold salted butter, diced
1 ¾ cups boiling water

Preparation
Grease a baking dish with butter. At 375 degrees F, preheat your oven. Place this pan on a baking sheet. Mix the melted butter with the brown sugar, vanilla, and

THE ULTIMATE IRISH COOKBOOK | 155

egg in a bowl. Stir in the half and half and mix evenly. Stir in the salt, flour, and baking powder and then mix until smooth. Fold in the chopped dates and spread the batter in a baking pan. Blend the brown sugar, boiling water, and butter in a bowl and pour over the cake. Bake for 40 minutes in the oven. Allow it to cool, slice, and serve.

Shamrock Cookies

Preparation time: 15 minutes
Cook time: 8 minutes
Nutrition facts (per serving): 289 Cal (13g fat, 3g protein, 2g fiber)

If you haven't tried the Irish shamrock cookies before, then here comes a simple and easy to cook recipe that you can recreate at home in no time with minimum efforts.

Ingredients (8 servings)

2 ½ cups all-purpose flour

2 teaspoon baking powder

1 teaspoon salt

1 cup unsalted butter

1 ½ cup confectioners' sugar

1 egg

2-3 teaspoon vanilla extract

½ cup semisweet chocolate chips

1 tablespoon shortening

½ cup green sprinkles

Preparation

At 400 degrees F, preheat your oven. Layer a baking sheet with parchment paper. Mix the flour with salt and baking powder in a bowl. Beat the butter with sugar, vanilla, and egg in a mixer. Stir in the flour mixture and mix evenly. Roll out the prepared dough on a floured surface into ¼ inch thick sheet. Cut the cookies using a cookie cutter and place them on a baking sheet. Bake the cookies for 8 minutes. Melt the semisweet chocolate chips with shortening in a bowl by heating in the microwave. Dip the top half of the cookies in the chocolate and allow it to set. Drizzle green sprinkles on top. Serve.

Irish Oat Flapjacks

Preparation time: 15 minutes
Cook time: 30 minutes
Nutrition facts (per serving): 250 Cal (6g fat, 12g protein, 10g fiber)

The famous oat flapjacks are essential to try on this Irish dessert menu. Try baking them at home with these healthy ingredients and enjoy them.

Ingredients (6 servings)

3 cups oatmeal

1 stick butter

⅓ cup light brown sugar

3 tablespoon golden syrup corn syrup

Preparation

At 350 degrees F, preheat your oven. Grease a 9x9 inches baking pan. Cook the golden syrup, brown sugar, and butter in a saucepan on low heat. Toss in the oats and mix well. Spread the oats mixture in the baking pan and bake for 30 minutes in the oven. Allow the baked flapjacks to cool and cut into bats. Serve.

Chocolate Pots De Crème

Preparation time: 15 minutes
Nutrition facts (per serving): 228 Cal (6g fat, 4g protein, 3g fiber)

Irish pots de crème is one good option to go for in the desserts. You can also keep them ready and stored, and then use them instead as instant desserts.

Ingredients (8 servings)
Pots de Crème
10 oz. semi-sweet chocolate chips
3 tablespoon granulated sugar
3 tablespoon Bailey's Irish Cream Liqueur
1 large egg
1 pinch of salt
1 cup heavy cream

Garnish
6 tablespoon Bailey's Irish Cream liqueur
Whipped Cream
Fresh mint sprigs
Cookies
Bailey's syrup

Preparation
Blend the chocolate with sugar, cream liqueur, egg, salt and cream in a blender for 1 minute. Divide the mixture in the serving bowls and top with cream liqueur, whipped cream, mint sprigs, and cookies. Finally, serve.

Irish Croissant Pudding

Preparation time: 10 minutes
Cook time: 55 minutes
Nutrition facts (per serving): 344 Cal (20g fat, 8g protein, 2.5g fiber)

Without this croissant pudding, it seems like the Irish dessert menu is incomplete. Try it with different variations of toppings.

Ingredients (6 servings)
Bread Pudding
6 croissants

2 cup half and half

4 eggs large

⅓ cup sugar

¼ teaspoon salt

1 teaspoon vanilla

¼ cup whiskey

1 cup raisins

1 tablespoon sugar sprinkle

Sauce
1 cup brown sugar packed

½ cup unsalted butter

2 tablespoon heavy whipping cream

Preparation
At 350 degrees F, preheat your oven. Grease 6 cup- a baking dish with cooking oil. Mix the whiskey with raisins in a bowl and leave for 10 minutes. Place the

croissants in a baking dish and spread the raisins mixture on top. Beat the half and half with vanilla, salt, lemon zest, sugar, and eggs in a bowl. Pour this mixture over the croissants and leave for 25 minutes. Drizzle the sugar on top and bake for 50 minutes at 350 degrees F. Allow the pudding to cool. For the sauce, mix all its ingredients in a saucepan and cook to a boil. Mix well and allow the sauce to cool. Pour the sauce over the pudding and garnish it with whipped cream. Serve.

Irish Rum Balls

Preparation time: 15 minutes
Cook time: 10 minutes
Nutrition facts (per serving): 255 cal (6g fat, 11g protein, 3g fiber)

Here's a delicious and savory combination of hazelnuts, chocolate, and sugar in the rum balls. All the right ingredients are mixed in a perfect balance to give you a great dessert.

Ingredients (6 servings)

7 tablespoon unsalted butter

¾ cup powdered sugar sieved

2 tablespoon rum

7oz. chocolate, chopped

7oz. peeled and toasted hazelnuts, ground

2 tablespoon cocoa powder

Preparations

Add chocolate to a bowl and melt by heating in the microwave. Toast the hazelnuts in a pan until golden and then grind in a food processor. Beat butter in a bowl until fluffy. Stir in powder sugar and beat again. Stir in the rum and mix well. Add the melted chocolate and mix until smooth. Add the ground hazelnuts, mix well, cover, and refrigerate for 30 minutes. Make small balls from this mixture and roll the balls in cocoa powder and powdered sugar. Serve.

Irish Whiskey Truffles

Preparation time: 10 minutes

Cook time: 5 minutes

Nutrition facts (per serving): 241 Cal (4g fat, 2g protein, 1.1g fiber)

Here comes a dessert that's loved by all. The whiskey truffles aren't only served as a dessert, but also as a famous snack in Ireland.

Ingredients (6 servings)

⅜ cups cream

3 tablespoon honey

1 shot any Irish whiskey

8 oz. dark chocolate

2 oz. soft butter

Cocoa powder, to dust

Preparation

Mix the whiskey with honey and cream in a suitable pot and cook to a boil. Remove from the heat and stir in the dark chocolate. Allow this mixture to cool. Blend with butter in a blender until smooth. Make small balls from this mixture and roll in cocoa powder. Serve.

Chocolate Guinness Cake

Preparation time: 5 minutes

Cook time: 50 minutes

Nutrition facts (per serving): 494 Cal (22g fat, 6g protein, 2g fiber)

Try the famous Irish chocolate Guinness cake with hints of vanilla. The combination is super refreshing and healthy.

Ingredients (6 servings)

1 cup Guinness

½ cup salted butter, cubed

2 cups sugar

¾ cup baking cocoa

2 large eggs, beaten

⅔ cup sour cream

3 teaspoon vanilla extract

2 cups all-purpose flour

1-½ teaspoon baking soda

Topping

1 package (8 oz.) cream cheese, softened

1-½ cups confectioners' sugar

½ cup heavy whipping cream

Preparation

At 350 degrees F, preheat your oven. Grease a 9-inch springform pan and layer with parchment paper. Mix the beer with the butter in a small saucepan and cook over low heat. Stir in the cocoa and sugar and then mix well. Remove from the heat and stir in the vanilla, sour cream, eggs, baking soda, and flour and then mix evenly. Spread this prepared batter in the pan and bake for 50 minutes. Allow the cake to cool. Beat the cream cheese with sugar and cream in a bowl until fluffy. Spread the frosting over the cake. Refrigerate for 1 hour, slice and serve.

Layered Mocha Brownies

Preparation time: 5 minutes
Cook time: 26 minutes
Nutrition facts (per serving): 295 Cal (14g fat, 2g protein, 1g fiber)

The Irish mocha brownies are loved by all due to their strong, refreshing taste and sweet flavors. Serve chilled for the best taste and unique flavor.

Ingredients (6 servings)
⅔ cup all-purpose flour
½ teaspoon baking powder
¼ teaspoon salt
⅓ cup butter
6 tablespoon baking cocoa
2 tablespoon canola oil
½ teaspoon instant coffee granules
1 cup sugar
2 large eggs, beaten
1 teaspoon vanilla extract

Frosting
2 cups confectioners' sugar
¼ cup butter, softened
3 tablespoon Irish cream liqueur

Ganache Topping
1 cup semisweet chocolate chips
3 tablespoon Irish cream liqueur

2 tablespoon heavy whipping cream

½ teaspoon instant coffee granules

Preparation

At 350 degrees F, preheat your oven. Mix the flour with salt and baking powder in a bowl. Mix the melted butter with coffee granules, oil, and cocoa in a bowl. Stir in the sugar and eggs and then mix evenly. Stir in the vanilla and flour mixture, mix evenly, and then spread the batter in an 8-inch pan. Bake it for 25 minutes. Meanwhile, beat all the frosting ingredients in a bowl and refrigerate for 1 hour. For the ganache, mix all its ingredients in a bowl and heat for 1 minute in a microwave on high heat. Spread the frosting over the cake and pour the ganache on top. Refrigerate for 1 hour and serve.

Caramel Whiskey Cookies

Preparation time: 10 minutes
Cook time: 9 minutes
Nutrition facts (per serving): 93 Cal (4g fat, 1g protein, 0g fiber)

The Irish whiskey cookies are great to serve on all the special occasions and festive dinners. They have these appealing caramel and chocolate toppings.

Ingredients (8 servings)
½ cup butter, softened
½ cup sugar
½ cup packed brown sugar
¼ cup plain Greek yogurt
2 tablespoon canola oil
1 teaspoon vanilla extract
2 ½ cups all-purpose flour
2 teaspoon baking powder
1 teaspoon baking soda
¼ teaspoon salt

Topping
24 caramels
1 tablespoon whiskey
3 oz. semisweet chocolate, melted
½ teaspoon salt

Preparation

At 350 degrees F, preheat your oven. Beat the butter with the sugars in a bowl. Stir in the yogurt, vanilla, and oil. Stir in the sugar mixture, baking soda, baking powder and flour before mixing evenly. Make 1-inch balls from this mixture. Spread the ball into two baking sheets and flatten them while making a dent at the center. Bake the cookies for 9 minutes and then allow them to cool. Melt the caramel in a bowl by heating in the microwave. Pour the caramel at the center of the cookies and drizzle salt and chocolate on top. Serve.

Drinks

Irish Creme Drink

Preparation time: 10 minutes
Nutrition facts (per serving): 218 Cal (8g fat, 4g protein, 1g fiber)

The Irish crème drink is famous for its blend of ice cream, vodka, eggnog, and milk. You can prep this drink easily at home.

Ingredients (4 servings)
3 ½ cups vanilla ice cream, softened
¾ cup vodka
½ cup eggnog
⅓ cup sweetened condensed milk
1 tablespoon chocolate syrup
1 teaspoon instant coffee granules
½ teaspoon vanilla extract
¼ teaspoon almond extract
Grated chocolate and chocolate syrup

Preparation
Blend the ice cream with rest of the ingredients in a blender. Garnish with chocolate and serve.

Irish Coffee

Preparation time: 5 minutes
Nutrition facts (per serving): 203 Cal (11g fat, 1g protein, 0g fiber)

The Irish coffee is all that you need to celebrate the winter holidays all year! Keep the drink ready in your refrigerator for quick serving.

Ingredients (2 serving)

2 teaspoon sugar
2 oz. Irish whiskey
2 cups hot strong brewed coffee
¼ cup heavy whipping cream
1 teaspoon green creme de menthe

Preparation

Beat the cream with the crème de menthe in a bowl. Divide the sugar and whiskey in two mugs. Add the cream mixture on top. Serve.

Guinness Float

Preparation time: 5 minutes
Nutrition facts (per serving): 286 Cal (7g fat, 4g protein, 1g fiber)

Here's a special Irish float drink made from ice cream, chocolate syrup, and Guinness. Slainte! Serve fresh for the best taste.

Ingredients (2 servings)

2 cup vanilla ice cream, softened

2 cups Guinness

2 tablespoon chocolate syrup

Preparation

Divide the ice cream in two glasses and top it with beer and chocolate syrup. Serve.

Irish Mule

Preparation time: 5 minutes
Nutrition facts (per serving): 207 Cal (1g fat, 1g protein, 1.3g fiber)

Made from Irish whiskey, ginger beer, and lime juice, this beverage is a refreshing addition to the Irish cocktail menu.

Ingredients (2 servings)

2 oz. Irish whiskey
6 oz. ginger beer
1 oz. lime juice
lime slices, for garnish
Mint sprig, for garnish
Ice

Preparation

Mix whiskey and the rest of the ingredients in a cocktail shaker. Next, garnish with mint, ice, and lime slices. Serve.

Irish Whiskey Cocktail

Preparation time: 10 minutes

Cook time: 30 minutes

Nutrition facts (per serving): 106 Cal (0g fat, 0g protein, 9g fiber)

This refreshing whiskey cocktail is always a delight to serve at parties. Now you can make it easily at home by using the following simple ingredients.

Ingredients (2 servings)

1 can Guinness Beer

½ cup sugar

2 cups water

½ cup honey

1 oz. lemon juice

1 ½ oz. honey simple syrup

3 oz. Jameson Irish Whiskey

4 mint leaves

Preparation

Mix the water, honey, and the rest of the ingredients in a cooking pan and cook for 30 minutes on a simmer. Allow the drink mixture to cool, strain, and serve.

If you liked Irish recipes, discover to how cook DELICIOUS recipes from **Balkan** countries!

Within these pages, you'll learn 35 authentic recipes from a Balkan cook. These aren't ordinary recipes you'd find on the Internet, but recipes that were closely guarded by our Balkan mothers and passed down from generation to generation.

Main Dishes, Appetizers, and Desserts included!

If you want to learn how to make Croatian green peas stew, and 32 other authentic Balkan recipes, then start with our book!

Order at www.balkanfood.org/cook-books/ for only $2,99

Maybe Hungarian cuisine?

If you're a **Mediterranean** dieter who wants to know the secrets of the Mediterranean diet, dieting, and cooking, then you're about to discover how to master cooking meals on a Mediterranean diet right now!

In fact, if you want to know how to make Mediterranean food, then this new e-book - "The 30-minute Mediterranean diet" - gives you the answers to many important questions and challenges every Mediterranean dieter faces, including:

- How can I succeed with a Mediterranean diet?
- What kind of recipes can I make?
- What are the key principles to this type of diet?
- What are the suggested weekly menus for this diet?
- Are there any cheat items I can make?

... and more!

If you're serious about cooking meals on a Mediterranean diet and you really want to know how to make Mediterranean food, then you need to grab a copy of "The 30-minute Mediterranean diet" right now.

Prepare **111 recipes with several ingredients in less than 30 minutes**!

Order at www.balkanfood.org/cook-books/ for only $2,99

What could be better than a home-cooked meal? Maybe only a **Greek** homemade meal.

Do not get discouraged if you have no Greek roots or friends. Now you can make a Greek food feast in your kitchen.

This ultimate Greek cookbook offers you 111 best dishes of this cuisine! From more famous gyros to more exotic *Kota Kapama* this cookbook keeps it easy and affordable.

All the ingredients necessary are wholesome and widely accessible.
The author's picks are as flavorful as they are healthy. The dishes described in this cookbook are "what Greek mothers have made for decades."

Full of well-balanced and nutritious meals, this handy cookbook includes many vegan options. Discover a plethora of benefits of Mediterranean cuisine, and you may fall in love with cooking at home.

Inspired by a real food lover, this collection of delicious recipes will taste buds utterly satisfied.

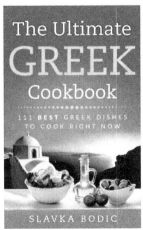

Order at www.balkanfood.org/cook-books/ for only $2,99

Maybe some Swedish meatballs ?

Maybe to try exotic **Syrian** cuisine?

From succulent *sarma*, soups, warm and cold salads to delectable desserts, the plethora of flavors will satisfy the most jaded foodie. Have a taste of a new culture with this **traditional Syrian cookbook**.

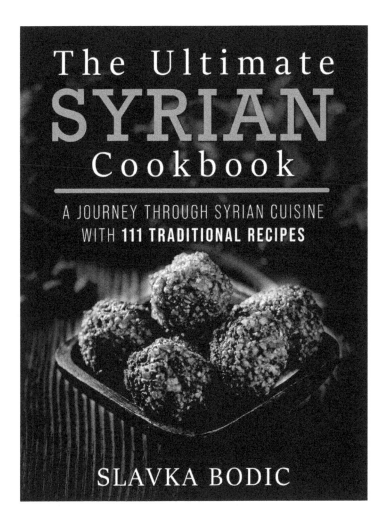

Order at www.balkanfood.org/cook-books/ for only $2,99

Maybe **Polish** cuisine?

Or **Peruvian**?

Order at www.balkanfood.org/cook-books/ for only $2,99

ONE LAST THING

If you enjoyed this book or found it useful, I'd be very grateful if you could find the time to post a short review on Amazon. Your support really does make a difference and I read all the reviews personally, so I can get your feedback and make this book even better.

Thanks again for your support!

Please send me your feedback at

www.balkanfood.org

Made in the USA
Middletown, DE
09 October 2023

40509108R00106